THE OBERON BOOK

OF

MODERN MONOLOGUES

FOR MEN

b

THE OBERON BOOK
OF
MODERN MONOLOGUES
FOR MEN

Chosen and Edited by Catherine Weate

OBERON BOOKS
LONDON

First published in 2008 by Oberon Books Ltd
521 Caledonian Road, London N7 9RH
Tel: 020 7607 3637 / Fax: 020 7607 3629
e-mail: info@oberonbooks.com
www.oberonbooks.com

A catalogue record for this book is available from the British Library.

ISBN: 9781-84002-825-6

Cover photograph by Anna Stephens: annastephensphotography.co.uk

Printed in Great Britain by CPI Antony Rowe, Chippenham.

Catherine has been voice coaching for over twenty years in England, Australia, Hong Kong and India. Her work has taken her into the diverse worlds of theatre, film, radio, education, commerce, law and politics. She has been Head of Voice at Rose Bruford College, Head of Voice and Vice Principal at the Academy of Live and Recorded Arts and Head of Examinations at LAMDA. Her other publications include *The Oberon Book of Modern Monologues for Women*, *The Oberon Book of Modern Duologues* and *Classic Voice (teaching vocal style)*.

INTRODUCTION

What a wonderful opportunity this has been to read through
significant numbers of plays published by Oberon Books. I've
discovered all sorts of playwrights that I'd never come across
before and a diverse range of fascinating and truly memorable
characters that cross cultural and historical boundaries. Their
stories range from the controversial (such as *Crossfire* by Michel
Azama, translated by Nigel Gearing, *Osama the Hero* by Dennis
Kelly, *Guardians* by Peter Morris, *Gladiator Games* by Tanika
Gupta and *Talking to Terrorists* by Robin Soans) to the comic (*A
New York Threesome: Madam Butterfly's Child* by Lesley Ross and
TRAGEDY: a tragedy by Will Eno).

Plenty of resource material for performance then, whether you're
an actor, director, student or teacher. To make reference easier
I've organised the monologues into age-specific groups: 'teens',
'twenties', 'thirties' and 'forties plus'. However, some of the
pieces aren't defined by age and cross a few of the boundaries
so do spend some time reading outside of your age related box,
just in case. Courage in *A Question of Courage* from *White Open
Spaces* could just as easily be in his thirties as in his twenties, for
example.

Monologue length varies widely depending on the material: the
concise and contained to the weighty and lengthy. I haven't cut
sections out of long speeches but left them intact in the hope that
someone somewhere will perform them whole. Don't be afraid
of adapting them to your needs however, particularly when many
auditions stipulate time frames for performance.

I'm hoping these monologues will inspire you to read further and discover more about the plays they come from. Not just to gain valuable insight into your character and the story they inhabit but for the sake of a thoroughly enjoyable (and sometimes confronting) read.

Catherine Weate

CONTENTS

PART FOUR: FORTIES PLUS

A list of the books from which these monologues are taken can be found on pages 163–6

PART ONE: TEENS

From

HELMET
by Douglas Maxwell

Helmet was first performed at the Traverse Theatre in a co-production between Paines Plough and the Traverse Theatre Company in March 2002.

Set in a computer games shop in Scotland, *Helmet* explores the worlds of Sal (a twenty-five year old Indian man who owns the shop) and RODDY a.k.a Helmet (a teenager who comes in regularly to play the games). The story is told in the style of a computer game where the characters have energy bars and three lives, which they can lose when their feelings are hurt, when things turn against them or if the energy bars fall below a certain level. This often means that scenes are replayed until the characters can solve the problem that caused them to lose a life. RODDY/HELMET is obsessed with computer games because they help him to escape from the real world. In this monologue, we begin to understand why.

RODDY

My wee brother Charlie died in a fire when he was only one.

It was thirteen days after my mum had gone. She left a note. She said good-bye to me but not my dad. She cried over Charlie's pram, then ran out the door without her coat on. She must have been cold.

My big brother Philip is in the army.

He came home when Dad got into trouble with the police for being sad. Philip's friend told him that Mum was in Girvan. Girvan has a beach and puggies and nothing else.

Dad took me and Charlie to Girvan in the car.

I had more room on the way back, but it took much longer.

We had a caravan on a hill and it smelt of pish. Me and Charlie stayed in the puggies when Dad was looking for Mum.

I played Sega Rally, Virtua Fighter, Star Wars Trilogy, Sensible Soccer, a flying game on a bike and House of the Dead with the gun. I said to Charlie that the arcade version is much better than the Saturn version. But he didn't know what I was talking about. He was only one.

On the second night Dad didn't come back. The woman from the caravan park told us that he'd phoned to say he'd be late. I was to give Charlie his dinner. But he didn't want that dinner. So I made chips.

After dinner I went to play Virtua Fighter in the puggies down at the harbour. I got to the second last level. A guy said

'You're really good at that game, wee man.' You're really good at that game, wee man.

When I got back the caravan was on fire and Charlie was in it.

I saw…

I saw…

I tried to drive the car to get Dad. But I couldn't do it. There were firemen and policemen and strangers but no-one could get Charlie out. He died in a fire and he was only one.

It was funny because Mum and Dad were there. But not in a nice way.

Dad never really spoke to Charlie, but he still tried to go into the fire to get him out.

I was in the car. I sat in the car and thought about Gran Turismo.

There's two hundred and fifty cars in Gran Turismo and full motion video replays. You have to get different licences and it's dead hard to get the A licence. There are no cheats available.

When I got home I had to see a counsellor. He let me play games in his office, but he never played. Except once and he couldn't do it. He didn't even know how to hold the controller. It's sad. But mostly he just wrote things down.

My brother Philip was crying on the phone. But not as much as Mum. He doesn't come back. Mum does. But not in a nice way.

I don't have a Playstation anymore. I don't have an N64. I don't have a megadrive. No SNES. No Gameboy. I don't have a Saturn or a Dreamcast.

I asked for a Playstation Two for my Christmas. But I didn't get it. I still buy the games though. I keep them in a box under my bed. Just in case.

Sometimes when you have no lives left, you play better. Because you know that if you make a mistake you die. You think faster and do things you didn't know you could do.

That's why I don't like those cheats that give you infinite lives. You don't get the feeling that you might die. Sometimes that's good. And sometimes that's bad.

But sometimes…sometimes the computer just decides to win. It just decides that you are going to die and it's not fair.

And there's nothing you can do about it.

You can be playing really well and not hurting anyone. Just lying there sleeping. And the game finishes.

All your lives are gone at once.

It's not fair.

And there's nothing you can do about it.

From

MANCUB

by Douglas Maxwell

(Adapted from the book *The Flight of the Cassowary* by John Levert)

Mancub *was commissioned by Vanishing Point and opened at the Traverse Theatre, Edinburgh in May 2005.*

PAUL is a Scottish teenager facing all the usual struggles of growing up. As his stresses increase, he retreats into the world of the animal kingdom. In this scene, PAUL talks to the audience about his struggle to approach girls and, for the first time, notices that people around him display the traits of certain animals.

PAUL

Walking home about 19 yards behind Karen. Watching every step. Every wiggle. Imagining the fabric around her body. Trying to remember her smell. Get it? Got it.

How do folk ask folk out? It's a mystery.

I can't speak to her face to face. That's insanity.

I can't phone her. That'd be worse. We've got one phone and it's in the kitchen. Everyone listens. If you're on for more than twenty-five seconds the King Of The Ants starts hopping in front of you pointing at his watch and miming money.

I can just imagine her

– guess which little fanny phoned up my house last night? I was like, no way man.

But it must happen somehow. People have girlfriends. Some people even have sex. They must do, I've seen it on TV.

She's surrounded by guys as always.

It reminds me of birds.

Male birds can only attract a female by showing off. Same as us. This school is an adolescent aviary.

The girls watch as we bump bellies and hop.

We have our crowing cockerels, our singing thrushes, our mocking mocking birds, a whole flock of us stomping the ground as the girls chew gum and send text messages.

I don't want any of that. I want to be an eagle. They don't dance or fight to get attention. They just circle, higher and higher, until they're a speck. Then they fold and plummet to the ground. Eyes wide open.

Faster faster faster faster

Closer closer closer closer

And just before they smash into the ground…wings…land…silent.

That would impress her. If I was an eagle.

From

RISK

by John Retallack

Risk *was first performed at the Tron Theatre, Glasgow, in February 2007. It is published in* Company of Angels, *which includes three other plays by John Retallack:* Hannah and Hanna, Club Asylum *and* Virgins.

Risk grew out of interviews with teenagers in Glasgow and explores why young people want to push boundaries and what they risk losing in the process. PAUL is fifteen years old and described as 'the Gambler', someone who 'takes bigger risks in order to come out on top'. He talks directly to the audience.

PAUL

I hate losing
I love winning

If I take a risk
I'm gonna take the biggest risk
Because if you're gonna get caught
You're as well getting caught for something major

D'y'know what I mean?

'What'd you get caught for?'
'Oh it was just a wee thing'
I think if you're gonna get caught
You've gotta get caught for something that's worth getting
caught for

Embarrassing to be caught for a wee thing.
You go down this road
You get caught for stealing a mars bar –
That's quite embarrassing

I'm not into scaring up some old lady
I want to go into something better than that
Something you go into smartly dressed
Somewhere you look the part an' all
A con artist
A manipulator
Up with the big boys really
Up with Mr Scorsese and his crew

I'm a learner
I'll take things on
But one thing I know –
The part of being caught
Isna' part of learning
Those who get caught
Are not very good at what they're doing

In order to succeed
Don't get caught.
If you get caught at something,
You've not thought it through enough.
You might want it
But you don't respect it.

If you don't get caught
You're doing something right.
Some birds are not meant to be caged
Their feathers are just too bright

It's so easy to make a bit o'extra money
A little deal here, a little deal there
You don't need a bank to break into
Or a train to hold up
Just be on hand for your friends
For their everyday needs.

If they want it
You provide it.
If they can't find it
You supply it.

If a stranger asks
Just deny it
It's so easy
If you plan ahead.

Analyse the situation
Weigh the odds
Don't rush
Keep breathing
Hold the eye
Smile, pocket, turn, and walk
Know when to disappear
Don't draw attention to yourself
Discreet you hear
DISCREET

From

CROSSFIRE
by Michel Azama, translated by Nigel Gearing.

This translation was first performed by Paines Plough at The Traverse Theatre, Edinburgh, in August 1993.

Crossfire explores how ordinary human beings are caught up in the atrocity of war. YONATHAN is fifteen years old and a foot soldier in a religious civil war. He finds himself pitched against one of his childhood friends, Ismail, who eventually shoots and kills him. This monologue, which he delivers just after his death, explains some of the horrors that he has had to confront. He speaks directly to the audience.

YONATHAN

They came to get me. They left me no choice.

Either you're with us or we take your gun away.

Taking my gun away would be like killing me. I said Okay.

I wanted to keep my distance stay out of it a bit.

The streets were blocked by jeeps with field-guns on them.

That part of town was sealed off we could cover the houses

from the motorway.

Heavy artillery on every hilltop.

They were like rats in a trap.

The people down below were waiting for the massacre.

Three whole days they waited like that for the massacre to

begin.

We pounded them with whole tons of bombs.

Our orders: liquidate. Liquidate all of them.

We killed in all sorts of ways.

M16s Kalashnikovs grenades machine-guns MPKs

rocket launchers anti-tank grenades chucked into the people

52 mortars Soviet rifles side-arms

even those stones you swing above your head at the end of a

piece of string. We killed with our bare hands.

You snap a man's neck you break backbones you

strangle with rope made of nylon you stab a knife in chests

you paralyse with a needle in the neck

with your knife you aim at arteries

and veins and under the collar-bone and of course at the heart.

It takes between ten seconds and three minutes for death to

happen.

There are some places to aim at which are really worth it the
eyes the genitals.
The eyes they're a doddle. The genitals they're tougher.
The guy it's like he feels he's fucking coming when you stick
your knife in his prick.
Not a pretty sight.
The most difficult thing to do is to cut the throat of a man
who's still alive.
You mustn't waste a single slash of the knife and it's best to do
it from behind.
Playing the hero is pointless.
We've booby-trapped cars doors cigarette-packets
jerrycans stuffed with TNT we've fired fired fired
even on kids because they grow up and one day
they'll shoot you in the back.
Helicopters dropped clusters of missiles
the camp burned the vines burned across miles of hills
stone-walls exploded
It only takes 48 hours and then you're finished with the
bombs the explosions the human pulp.
Hang on in there hang on in there just a bit further till the end
whole bunches of kids would throw themselves under the
tanks
they were crushed to death whole groups of them
others set on fire with flame-throwers
human torches still running for another hundred yards.
All for one more second of life.
Blood filling your hands clothes eyes walls.
Slaughter slaughter slaughter.

KERPOW! The other guy falls you step over him you don't
see anything any more you move forward a corpse falls on
top of you explodes into bits and pieces all cut to shreds and
splashing you in a shower of blood.
At every step children in little bits babies their heads
bust open
disembowelled women holding on to their children
you're like an animal it's them or you
fire – bang! – at anything that moves a kid a cat a pal.
Bang bang bang save your skin bang bang bang bang.

From

PLAYING FIELDS
by Neela Dolezalova

Playing Fields *was first performed at Soho Theatre, London in October 2002.*

JUSTIN is sixteen years old and has just learnt that he is going to be a father. He only slept with Thyme once and was too insecure to return her calls. Now three months pregnant, Thyme is in a relationship with a girl, Felicity (Flea). The two girls have been busy fighting for the survival of the local playing fields in North London. Thyme is at her cousin Pete's flat when JUSTIN turns up unexpectedly to smoke a joint with Pete. Before announcing that she is pregnant, Thyme baits JUSTIN a little and suggests that he needs saving just as much as the playing fields (JUSTIN's father used to be violent). Thyme leaves and JUSTIN is left to explain himself to Pete. The two boys are alone. Pete has just hit him.

JUSTIN

You have no idea do you? No idea what this bitch has done.
Bitch gone and fucked up my life that's what. What's my dad
gonna say? He'll fucking laugh that's what. And do you know
how that'll feel, huh?

No reply.

I don't wanna end up like him. I'm changing it Pete. Don't
you understand?

No reply.

My kids are gonna have the fucking world. My kids are gonna
live like princes. Trust me. I can't do that now. I can't give
them what I've promised them. Thyme don't realise what
she's saying by telling me I'm a father. I'm not a father until
I've learnt more and sorted myself out in here. I promised
myself that Pete. I promised. I didn't promise it *for* myself,
I did it so that my kids will have a better fucking chance
than me, so that I don't fuck them up. Can't you see the
difference?

No reply.

What do you want me to say? I ain't got nothing more to say.

Longish pause.

Why'd she care so much about a field? Hey? What's a field
when she's got a kid growing insider her? What was she trying
to do? Bitch was trying to make me angry that's what. I bet
she wanted me to hit her. I bet she wanted me to get angry

and beat her to fucking pulp. Beat that baby right out of her body so she can blame it all on me.

Slight pause.

Look what you done Justin, you just killed your own kid. She just wanted me to get angry, she made me shout at her so that she can say I ain't fit to be a dad. What the fuck would she know? One day I'll be the best father anyone could have.

Pause.

I'd never hit my kids. My kids are gonna live like princes.

From

VIRGINS
by John Retallack

Virgins *was first performed at the Junction Theatre, Cambridge, in July 2006. It is published in* Company of Angels, *which includes three other plays by John Retallack:* Hannah and Hanna, Club Asylum *and* Risk.

Virgins is described as a 'family drama about sexual politics', which explores some of the issues surrounding teenage sexual experimentation. Seventeen year old JACK is home from a party where he took drugs and had (unprotected) sex for the first time. Unfortunately he can't remember much about it at all. He speaks directly to the audience.

JACK

I'm trying to behave as normally as I can
So that Mum and Dad won't ask too many questions
When they get up

It's Sunday and I'm at home

Right now I am on a totally different planet to everyone else

I woke up in the front garden at six
I don't know how I got there
I got to my bed without disturbing the snores from their
room.

When I woke up
I never felt so bad in my life
My heart was really pounding
I thought I'd faint
Then I felt so sick
I couldn't stand I was so dizzy

I'm up now and I'm practising being normal
But I'm not normal
Not anymore

Last night is a complete blank
Except for one thing
I had sex
I had sex with Sadie Bennett on the floor of the bathroom at
the party
Sadie Bennett

I had sex with Sadie Bennett

I've always fancied her
And she was there!
I was away, I was flying, I mean I was totally out my skin
And we danced and she laughed at everything I said
And she was well gone too
And I just knew it was on
At last
I knew it

And then what?

Oh God...

What happened after?

What the hell happened next?

From

PRIVATE PEACEFUL

by Michael Morpurgo, adapted by Simon Reade

Private Peaceful *was first performed in April 2004 at Bristol Old Vic's Studio Theatre.*

This play is based on Michael Morpurgo's moving tale about seventeen year old TOMMO PEACEFUL, who spends his last night during World War I reliving the events that led him to this juncture in time. Here he remembers, for the audience, a tense moment in trench warfare.

TOMMO

Word has come down from headquarters that we must send out patrols to find out what regiments have come into the line opposite us. Why we have to do this we do not know – there are spotter planes doing it almost every day. My turn soon comes up. Charlie's too. Captain Wilkie's heading the patrol and he tells us 'we have to bring back a prisoner for questioning'. He gives us a double rum ration, and I'm warmed instantly to the roots of my hair, to my very toenails.

On the signal, we climb over the top and crawl on our bellies through the wire.

We snake our way forward. It takes an eternity to cross no-man's-land. I begin to wonder if we'll ever find their trenches at all. We slither into a shell hole and lie doggo there for a while. We can hear Fritz talking now, and laughing – and playing music.

Sound: a distant gramophone plays.

We're close now, very close. I'm not scared – I'm excited. I'm out poaching with Charlie. I'm tensed for danger.

Then we see the wire up ahead. We wriggle through a gap and drop down into their trench.

It looks deserted, but we can still hear the voices and the music. I notice the trench is much deeper than ours, wider too and more solidly constructed. I grip my rifle tight and follow Charlie along the trench, bent double like everyone else.

(*TOMMO.*) We're making too much noise. I can't understand why no one has heard us. Where are their sentries, for God's sake?

At that moment, a German soldier comes out of a dug-out. For a split-second the Hun does nothing and neither do we. We just stand and look at one another. Then he lets out a shriek, blunders back into the dug-out. I don't know who threw the grenade in after him, (*Sound: blast.*) but there is a blast that throws me back against the trench wall. There is screaming and firing from inside the dug-out. Then silence. The music has stopped.

From

OSAMA THE HERO
by Dennis Kelly

Osama the Hero *was initially written and developed as part of the Paines Plough's Wild Lunch 2004. It was first produced by the Hampstead Theatre in London in May 2005.*

GARY is seventeen years old and sees the world differently to everybody else at his school and on the estate where he lives. This speech, directed to the audience, explains one of his most controversial views. Unfortunately there has been some violence on the estate and GARY is an easy target to blame.

GARY

Find a hero, a living hero, presentation on a contemporary hero, but it has to be someone who's truly heroic, someone who's an inspiration to millions, a determined individual who'll sacrifice wealth, life and happiness for what they believe in and I scrabble around, I try, I try really hard, no-one, nothing, celebrities, politicians, sportspersons, but to be honest there's nothing, there's nothing, there's nothing and suddenly I find one: BANG! Inspiration, lightning bolt, epiphany, perfect sense. I'm standing in front of the class and I read out the title of my project:

'Osama the Hero.'

And I'm telling them, I'm telling them, I'm telling them about a boy, as a young man, twenty-two years old rejecting his family's vast personal fortune, three billion dollars and off into the mountains of Afghanistan to fight the communists, but really, not fight in the way our leaders fight, but really fight and get wounded, not fight like a president or a prime minister, sending boys off to slaughter each other while you eat in the best restaurants and go to concerts and think about what you'll spend your money on when you retire, but go out there with a gun and fight yourself, bleeding, injured, I tell them of a quiet man who rarely laughs but often smiles, who lives simply, eats simply, dresses simply, according to those who have met him a man of impeccable manners who is known never to lie, I explain how despite being on the run in one of the world's poorest regions this man is so well loved that no-one has turned him in to claim the fifty million dollar reward, I explain how this man survived a war against the greatest powers on earth with only a few hundred fighters and little resources and then I look up. And I see the faces. Staring at me. They're just staring at me. Worse than before. This time. This time. This time I know I've really done something.

From

BLUE

by Ursula Rani Sarma

Blue *was commissioned by the Cork Opera House in 2000 and was first performed in the Half Moon Theatre in June 2000.*

DES is in his late teens and lives in an isolated sea-side town in Ireland. It is his very last day of school and important swimming heats are about to take place the following day. If he wins a medal he has a chance of securing a scholarship to Berkley so he decides to skip a soccer match to train. Here he explains to the audience how he is caught by one of the teachers.

DES

Outside the day is so beautiful I want to cry,
the road is hot already,
sticking tar to the soles of my shoes,
I turn out from our gate and see her there before me,
all shimmering and shining in her milky blues and greens,
We have grey summers here,
but not today, look at it,
they won't do a tap in the school
last day today and they'll only be giving awards for the
best footballer and the best hurler,
the exams though,
I get a burning in my chest when I think about them,
but it's the last day though,
and the heats are tomorrow.

I go straight for the pool,
I can see the lads are all only down the strand anyway.
Playing soccer,
I want to train,
I strip to my shorts and there's no one there but me.
The water's like a sheet,
I dive through and start to stroke.
Find the rhythm.
Two hundred per cent in the water, two hundred percent
concentration.
Cut through the water like a knife.
Feel my body change gears like an engine and this is it,
I feel it.

This is the first day of something else.

I'm well into it now,
must be on my twentieth lap or so,
when I see him standing at the side of the pool,
my lungs freeze,
he doesn't look happy.
I swim to the side and
'good morning sir,
No sir,
what?
Special, sir, no I don't think I'm special it's just with the
heats tomorrow I –
But I don't play soccer I –
And with three words he shatters everything that was
perfect about today,
Off the team
But I'm team captain sir –
It's tomorrow sir,
the medal, the scholarship,
You can't do that sir'

From

FAITH

by Meredith Oakes

Faith *was first performed at the Royal Court Theatre Upstairs, London, in October 1997.*

PRIVATE LEE FINCH is nineteen years old and a British soldier stationed in the South Atlantic during the Falklands Island conflict. LEE, his sergeant and some other soldiers have been billeted in a remote farmhouse and are engaged in combat for possession of one of the islands. His sergeant is just not capable of inspiring the men and spends a great deal of his time trying to stay out of the action. LEE explains to Sandra, the farmhouse owner, why sergeants are different from other soldiers.

LEE

Sergeants are so boring, everyone hates them. Everyone hates them cause everyone wants to be mad. And sergeants want to be sane. They want to be sane so badly. They wind up being madder than all the rest of us put together.

They have to train us to be hard, see, which means they have to be hard on us. There was one used to get me up five o'clock every morning my first three weeks. Out running before the sun came up, all round the barracks with ice all over the roads and they'd be shouting at us how we were the worst they'd ever had, so weak, no puff, they were all day telling me how thick I was and I'd never make it, it's just, I like to stop and think but you're never supposed to, so they're all the time making out I'm a halfwit because I have thoughts.

They break you right down, they make sure you know exactly how bad life can be when they don't respect you, nothing you do seems to please them and they make you feel like a boil on the face of the earth. Then one day you do something right and someone gives you a good word suggesting they don't hate you quite as much as before. So then the joy of living starts up again, it's like you're born again and they've become your parents, a few weeks down the line and by then you're well in. You're not allowed home the first six weeks. They know what they're doing see. By that time they've become your family, you've won the acceptance and you're really happy they let you belong. Only that's why it comes as a bit of a shock when they let you go off and get killed, because families aren't supposed to be like that.

But this is the sergeant's problem. Because the reason he takes the trouble to be hard on you is that he cares. The more he cares, the more he treats you like a bastard. The more he treats you like a bastard, the more he cares. I don't think it's good for them. They get really strange, some of them. They get really nice to you. It's horrible.

PART TWO: TWENTIES

From

CRESSIDA AMONG THE GREEKS
by David Foley

Cressida Among the Greeks *was first performed at the Ohio Theatre in New York City in February 2002.*

Around 1250 BC the city of Troy was under siege from the Greek army. In this version of Shakespeare's *Troilus and Cressida*, American playwright, David Foley, explores love and betrayal amidst the chaos of this siege. Here, HECTOR, a member of the royal family in the city of Troy, has just returned from a battle and explains to his family how he thought he had killed the great Greek warrior Achilles.

HECTOR

It was Achilles. I know the chariot. I know the shield. I know the insignia of his father's house. It was Achilles. I knew him. And he knew me – though two armies rode between us.

But he was coy – or clever. Rode just behind the lines. Just where I could see him but couldn't – get at him. I went after him. A man tried to bar my way. I spitted him on my spear and flung him behind me. Another tried to climb aboard my chariot. I split his head open with my sword. But still he kept his distance. Riding away just behind the lines. Taunting me.

I was in a fury. I redoubled my attack – killing, crushing – I hardly knew what I was doing anymore. I only wanted to get at him.

And suddenly I did. I was there, and on the open field there was just him and me. This seemed to startle him. He lost his nerve or something. Made one turn too many or too sharp and was thrown from his chariot. I hurled myself after him – grappled him right there on the ground. His sword came up and slammed against my head, stunned me, and in just that moment, he got the better of me. He reared up over me, his spear raised for the final thrust.

But he was careless. He raised his arms too high, and I thrust up with my sword – caught him just under the chin, sliced right up through the jaw and tongue and brain. His blood rained down and blinded me and I rolled free as he toppled in the mud.

I couldn't believe it! I'd got him at last! Achilles! The pride and terror of the Greeks. It seemed too simple. I went to him. I reached to claim his helmet for my trophy. I tore it off. It was – It was –

It was not – Achilles – It was –

Patroclus.

Yes. Patroclus. He'd sent the boy – his lover – out, dressed in his own armor – Why? To tease me? Bait me? Draw me on? Why? Why?

From

THE DARKER FACE OF THE EARTH
by Rita Dove

The Darker Face of the Earth, *by the former US Poet Laureate, was first performed at the Oregon Shakespeare Festival in Ashland, Oregon, USA in July 1996 and in the United Kingdom at the Royal National Theatre in August 1999.*

The Darker Face of the Earth is an updated version of the Oedipus story but set on a plantation in South Carolina in the 1840s. Amalia Jennings is the wife of the plantation owner and twenty years ago she gave birth to a son by a black slave. The child was smuggled out of the plantation in a wicker sewing basket and is believed dead. However, AUGUSTUS didn't die and has recently been bought as a slave by the same plantation. Nobody knows, including AUGUSTUS, that Amalia is his mother. Lonely and neglected by her husband, Amalia invites him up to the house where they talk about slavery. AUGUSTUS tells the following story, which helps ignite Amalia's admiration and passion.

AUGUSTUS

Now I have a story for you.
Once there was a preacher slave
went by the name of Isaac.
When God called him
he was a boy, out hunting ricebirds.
Killing ricebirds is easy –
just pinch off their heads.

   Indicating the sherry.

May I?

   AMELIA *flinches, nods. He pours the sherry expertly.*

But one day, halfway up the tree
where a nest of babies chirped,
a voice called out: "Don't do it, Isaac."
It was an angel, shining
in the crook of a branch.
Massa let him preach.
What harm could it do?

   Sitting down in the damask chair.

Then a slave uprising in Virginia
had all the white folks
watching their own niggers
for signs of treachery.
No more prayer meetings, Isaac!
But God would not wait,
so Isaac kept on preaching
at night, in the woods.

Of course, he was caught.
Three of his congregation
were shot on the spot, three others branded
and their feet pierced.
But what to do about Isaac,
gentle Isaac who had turned traitor?

First they flogged him. Then
they pickled the wounds with salt water,
and when they were nearly healed,
he was flogged again, and the wounds
pickled again, and on and on for weeks
while Massa sold off Isaac's children
one by one. They took him to see
his wife on the auction block,
baby at her breast.
A week later it was his turn.
His back had finally healed;
but as his new owner led him
from the auction block,
Isaac dropped down dead.

   Pause; more to himself than to AMALIA.

They couldn't break his spirit,
so they broke his heart.

From

CAR

by Chris O'Connell

Car was first performed by Theatre Absolute, in co-production with the Belgrade Theatre, on 22 June 1999, in Coventry's Transport Museum. The play transferred to the Pleasance Theatre for the 1999 Edinburgh Festival and won the Scotsman Fringe First Award for outstanding new work. After transferring to the Pleasance Theatre, London, Car was awarded a Time Out Live Award – Best New Play on the London Fringe, 1999.

The play opens with the violent theft of a car by four boys. One of the boys, JASON, is in his early twenties, and, despite injuring the owner of the car, is exhilarated by the crime. JASON owes money to his drug dealers, and, fuelled by an adrenaline rush from the car theft, murders someone at their request. Here, he speaks to two of the other boys, Tim and Mark, about how his actions have changed his life forever.

JASON

The car? the car, the car, the car, the car, the car, the car, the car, the car, the car, the car, I noticed...it's red. My old man, he drives a red car. He's always driven red cars. In Japan, so he tells me, they drive white cars. Drive red cars and you're not trustworthy. My dad travels abroad and he always comes back with presents for me and my sister and he kisses my mum like he's missed her, like he's really missed her, and then he kisses me and my sister, he gets tears in his eyes and they glisten, you know when mercury breaks out of a thermometer, like it's had too much telling to do and it sends its drops, one, two, three, four, solid drops down to the floor. My dad's tears; like a mercury drop. And we're all happy to be together. We're a family on a beach, holding hands and sharing jokes. My dad tells a joke and I look up at him, I like the way his face spreads when he smiles. In my head, I'm on the beach a million times a day and the happiness gets infectious. I'm desperate for it. Beach life; give me that happy life on the beach. But then in the Crown tonight, pulling the trigger, the beach falls in and my whole life pours into the egg timer hole left gaping in the crust of the earth. Everything's changed, forever.

JASON sinks to the floor.

From

KID

by Chris O'Connell

Kid was produced by Theatre Absolute, in co-production with the Belgrade Theatre, Coventry. It was previewed on 15 July 2003, at the Belgrade Theatre Within a Theatre. The play subsequently transferred to the Edinburgh Fringe Festival, premiering at the Pleasance Cavern.

K has had a difficult life, in and out of prison for petty crimes. After beating a boy to death he flees the country and ends up backpacking in Central America. A year later he returns to his friend Lee, and Lee's pregnant girlfriend Zoe, who both witnessed the murder. Zoe doesn't want K back in their lives as she prepares for the birth of her child: being pregnant has changed everything for her. Here, K explains to Lee and Zoe the circumstances that turned his life around.

K

When I first got there, I was in the capital. I couldn't stand it, crappy hotels, the heat, too much noise. I headed towards the country. I didn't know where I was going to stay, but there was just this sun, warm. I talked to people I didn't know. I started cleaning shoes.

And this guy I meet, he sells bits of fruit and vegetables outside his house, he gets a spare room cleaned up for me. Every day I go and collect the milk. He's got three goats.

It's a walk past this big chocolate coloured mountain I can see, way off. I've started to look at it, I've thought how it belongs to me. Night times, I end up working on a fishing boat, just bobbing in the harbour, cleaning the nets. I can't speak the language, but this old woman, she tells me a few words. I went to school until I was sixteen, yeah, I leave and I can hardly read and write, I spend ten months in this village and I've learnt a lifetime. (*Beat.*) Nearly killed me.

Being out there. There was a storm, from the mountains. I never heard anything like it.

It's hard to describe. A whole day, rumbling, and then it rained, three days of rain, and then this flood sweeping through the village. The flood's rolling down that mountain I've been watching. I've called it The Nest cos of the birds I've seen swirling round the peak. But then it's death mountain. I call it Death Mountain cos it's pouring this mud and this water.

But the rain's not stopping, and I see these taxi drivers, they always wait outside the post office, the policeman, (*To* ZOE.) the craft stalls where I got that toy, the kids crossing from the school, do you know what I mean? They're all swept away.

Yeah. I'm like you, I can't believe it, and I'm watching it. I grab onto a tree, and then I leg it down towards the square cos I can hear people screaming, crying. I'm running faster than the mud slide.

There's houses down the main street, cracking, like my leg when I was thirteen… It's mad, yeah?… And I get to the square and there's loads of people. Some of them I know, I've polished their shoes, and they're splashing up and down, they're drowning. I want to leg it again. It's too big for me. I stare at them, they're reaching out. Like this… Like this… (*Beat.*) I saw a kid floating on its back, getting dragged under by the current. Suddenly, I dived in and I got it, then it flipped out of my hands. She went under. I got her again, held her up, like this. I felt sick. I felt myself going under, I got a mouthful of mud, water, two, three; suddenly I couldn't stay up.

I'm a cunt Lee. All my life, people hating the cunt in me. It's in my head, and I don't want the kid to go under with me. I don't want to die, not now. (*Silence.*) I grabbed her. I pulled her up onto the bank. Held her.

From

KINGS OF THE ROAD
by Brian McAvera

Kings of the Road *was first performed at the Old Museum Arts Centre in May 2002. Produced by Directions Out Production Company for Littoral Arts, as part of the Routes Festival, in association with Cathedral Arts Festival.*

TJ is unconscious in a hospital bed after the bus on which he worked was blown up during the Troubles in Northern Ireland. His son, RINTY, is at his side and he recalls the stories of three generations of bus workers in their family, helped by the ghost of his grandfather. In this scene, RINTY replays the moment when he had turned twenty and explained to his father why he wanted to work on the buses.

RINTY

Da.

You know why I want to go on the buses, don'tcha?

The real reason?

Something Grandad said.

An' then you told me it later.

Frankie Carson Da.

On his retirement.

Remember you told me.

Frankie saying there was this wee girl, used to get on his bus when he first started.

And he watched her, Madeleine was her name, grow up.

Watched her courtin' with her husband-to-be.

Watched her kids grow up, her on the bus with her pram.

An' every time he seen her out walking with the pram, and he in the bus, he'd beep the horn an' wave at her, and she'd always wave back.

An' when Frankie retired, she went all over the town, looking fer him, found his depot, and got his address.

An' she knocked on his door and she said:

'Frankie Carson, I'm the one's been looking fer you.

I grew up with you, on the buses, and this is fer you.'

An' she handed him this lovely card and inside, there were two ten pound vouchers for Marks and Spencers.

An' she saw him looking at them, and she said, 'I'm sorry I can't afford any more Mister Carson, but if I win the Freestate lottery, I know where you live!'

(*A beat.*) I want a job like that Da.

Where people remember you like that... Da...

Just like Grandad... Just like you...

From

KISS ME LIKE YOU MEAN IT
by Chris Chibnall

Kiss Me Like You Mean It *was first performed at Soho Theatre
and Writers' Centre in May 2001*

TONY meets Ruth for the first time outside of a party in
Manchester at 3.00 a.m. on a hot midsummer's night and is
instantly attracted to her. Meanwhile, Don and Edie, who are
in their seventies and live on the floor above, are having a party
of their own. TONY and Ruth are drawn into their world and,
Don advises TONY to 'grab life by the collar'. Here, TONY takes
a deep breath and tells Ruth exactly how he feels.

TONY

Listen… I need to… Um… Say… I mean… I know we only met earlier… And I nearly set you on fire… And we're both going out with people. Obviously that's quite tricky. But… Well… You are the most beautiful woman I have ever laid eyes on in my entire life. I saw you and my heart leapt. You make me want to change my life. To…participate. I know it's not possible and that you have a boyfriend and we're not… compatible or whatever but… I just… I know it's stupid…but maybe just hear me out for a second and then you can tell me I'm an idiot and we'll both go back in and pretend this never happened but… I want to travel the world with you. I want to bring the ice cold Amstel to your Greek shore. And sit in silence and sip with you. I want to go to Tesco's with you of a Sunday. Watch you sleep, scrub your back, rub your shoulders, suck your toes. I want to write crap poetry about you, lay my coat over puddles for you, always have a handkerchief available for you. I want to get drunk and bore my friends about you, I want them to phone up and moan about how little they see me because I'm spending so much time with you. I want to feel the tingle of our lips meeting, the lock of our eyes joining, the fizz of our fingertips touching. I want to touch your fat tummy and tell you you look gorgeous in maternity dresses, I want to stand next to you wide-eyed and hold my nose as we open that first used nappy, I want to watch you grow old and love you more and more each day. I want to fall in love with you. I think I could. And I think it would be good. And I want you to say yes. You might feel the same.

Beat.

Could you? Maybe?

From

BEST MAN SPEECH
by Glyn Maxwell

This play was first performed as The Best Man *in August 2004 at the Smirnoff Underbelly, Edinburgh.*

BAILEY is the disillusioned and downtrodden best man of bridegroom Addy and takes revenge in his 'Best Man Speech' with some serious revelations about his so-called friend. This monologue has been taken from the start of the speech and BAILEY has a large wrapped present in front of him.

BAILEY

Well. This is the present. Get it? Present.
I expect you've all had presents
you'd rather not have had. This is the present
I've sort of dreaded. This is the present moment.
And me, well I'm the best man they could find.
Miranda and Addy. Addy, friend of my youth,
and I wish you'd leave my youth alone, he's shy,
and Miranda, blushing bride, only not blushing,
congratulations, may you – blush forever.
Blushing best man, it ought to say. It's me
alone in the present moment, I'm the one
the light's caught. You can't stop me,
can you, it's my moment.

Look at the lovely bridesmaids. Don't they look
lovely. They're not blushing either. Sammie,
Jade, and Tabitha. On their behalf
I answer the toast, I answer the toast. Hey, toast,
the answer's no. You're going in the toaster.
That was my first joke.
(It says here: 'Wait for laughter to die down.')
Splendid. On we go.

Now. You're probably wondering about my present,
my humble offering to the happy couple.
There's a prize for guessing what's inside. Clue:
it's a high-tech device for *easy listening*.
State of the art. I tell you, cutting-edge,
it'll blow you away, trust me. Now, who am I…

I should have started there, my mother did.
My name is Bailey. I do have a first name,
but they took it at the door. I've got this ticket
to get it back, but till that time, I'm Bailey.
It's simpler for Addy, that, just the one name.
Some of you regulars at this élite
venue, the Maple Vale Country Club,
might know me by my other name of 'Barman,
where's my bloody lager?' or perhaps
'Oi, caddie, that's a friggin' five-iron!' Well,
caddie, barman, waiter,
those are my slave names. But for once I'm here,
in with the cream. I ought
by rights to raise a glass to the supremo
who made the Maple Vale Country Club
what it is today, but as you know,
he happens to be the groom, and he's had enough
compliments for one day, though, having said that,
mostly in his own speech. So I'll merely
thank the staff on duty here today,
(suckers, having to clear up after this lot,
whoops, there goes some more)

   He throws his drink over his shoulder.

and say how very pleased I am to be
among what we always call 'the bastard public'.
(Shouldn't have said that, Addy, should I, no,
looked good on paper.) Anyway, I'm speaking,
I have the floor. Yes, I hear him going,
you'll be mopping it this time tomorrow, Bailey.

From

THE GOD BOTHERERS
by Richard Bean

The God Botherers *was first performed at The Bush Theatre,*
London in November 2003.

The play takes place in a mythical African Muslim country
called Tambia, where Laura, a young English woman, arrives
to undertake foreign aid work. MONDAY is a Tambian and is
assigned to look after Laura, given the restrictions and dangers
facing women there. He is presented as an opportunist whose
ambition is to buy the permitted three wives; however he is
also torn between different religions and eventually gets on
the wrong side of the local fundamentalists. Here, he reveals
(to the audience) his thoughts about religious confrontation
through the story of his ancestor.

MONDAY

Wale Adenuga, my father's father's grandfather, was not a
warrior, he was a story teller, and the first man in Unoka to
see an iron cow. He told this story every week of his life and
he was still telling it on the day they carried him back into the
forest to sleep the long sleep. He was weeding his land when
he heard a strange thunder. He called the Poro and they came
with their machetes. A white man came out of the forest
riding on a great iron cow. The white man could not speak
properly and had a Kebbe man with him to change his words.
'There is only one God,' said the white man, 'and he gave
us a son, Jesus Christ, who is also a God, a God who is both
man and god, and then there is the Holy Ghost. You must not
worship false gods, and it is wrong to eat human flesh.' The
Poro warriors wanted to kill the white man but Wale Adenuga
knew that he could destroy the white man with words. 'You
say there is only *one* God. And this "One God" has a son
called Jesus, who is also a God. Things must be different
where you come from, because here, in Unoka, one and one
makes two.' The Poro had never laughed so loud. The white
man turned red, and they had never seen skin change colour,
so they laughed even harder, and Wale Adenuga with skill was
riding the laughter like a snake on the white water. 'And this
brother of the One and only God, the quiet one, the Holy
Ghost, he must be a god too, so that's three gods, and the big
One God if he has a son, must have a wife, who would have to
be a god too, because the big One God would not want to lay
down with the daughter of a yam farmer. So that is four gods
already, but wait, I need a piss!' And Wale Adenuga walked

over to the iron cow and pissed against the wheels, and as he pissed he carried on counting, 'four, five, six gods, seven' and all the Poro laughed, and no work at all was done that day in the fields, and the women were brought together and Wale Adenuga was made to tell the story again and again, until he fell down drunk from palm wine and happiness.

(*Beat.*) Three market weeks later the white man returned with warriors wearing coats made of blood. They went into the bush to where the young Poro were living, and learning the ways of the forest. Twenty-three were killed. The Poro collected their bodies and ate their hearts so that their power was not wasted and today their spirits live on, and they are forever with the Kebbe.

From

GUARDIANS
by Peter Morris

Guardians *premiered in August 2005 on the Edinburgh Fringe,*
and received a 2005 Fringe First Award. The play was staged
at the Pleasance Cavern by the Mahwaff Theatre Company.

Guardians presents a series of alternating monologues by two
characters called THE ENGLISH BOY and The American Girl,
who present their stories directly to the audience. The common
thread through both sets of speeches is a series of photos
depicting Iraqi prisoner abuse. THE ENGLISH BOY is an Oxbridge
educated, tabloid journalist in his twenties. While trolling a gay
sadomasochistic club he meets a submissive boy, who spends
time in the Territorial Army. He provides THE ENGLISH BOY
with an opportunity to manufacture photographs depicting
British soldiers abusing Iraqi prisoners in order to further his
career in journalism.

THE ENGLISH BOY

Now I have to say that, in spite of what might seem my near-lecherous enthusiasm for it, what I do is a job like any other. I mean, it's rather dull sometimes. Much of the time.

The worst is Picture Captions. At this stage of the game, I can't escape doing them – someone's got to. But still, it's fucking dull. Example: magazine pre-releases a pic, hoping to boost sales for their next issue. They send it to us, our readers like a bit of vacuous totty – then I'm left to dream up a caption. *'You're-A-Vision! Pop contest hopeful Whatsername is set to represent the UK: here, she strips off for FHM.'*

You see what I've done there? It's a pun. 'You're-A-Vision'? Obviously that's crap, but it's the only way to amuse yourself – if not others – when you're the bastard writing the captions.

My difficulty is – well. I find myself staring at the photos and – and trying to work out what to say. Or why. Or how a tabloid newspaper can convey any meaning, as you leaf through and see it all, the tits and the footballers, the toddlers with cancer and the waitress who tells all about her kinky romp with the Chuckle Brothers – all of this beside a photo of – of something important. Something that's meant to mean something. But in this context, what possible context can you give it? With just a handful of words, printed under a photo of –

Listen. I'm not trying to sound wanky about it. I mean, I've made it sound like some sort of metaphysical dilemma but...but like I said, it's a job like any other, with rules.

From

A QUESTION OF COURAGE
by Courttia Newland from
White Open Spaces

White Open Spaces *was produced by Pentabus Theatre in partnership with BBC Radio Drama. It was first performed in preview at The Courtyard Theatre, Hereford in July 2006 and opened at The Pleasance King Dome, Edinburgh Festival Fringe in August 2006.*

White Open Spaces is a series of seven monologues about racism in the English countryside. They were inspired by Trevor Phillips, Chair of the Commission for Racial Equality, who asked if the countryside was guilty of 'passive apartheid' back in 2004. In *A Question of Courage* a couple from London, COURAGE (black) and Myrna (white) spend some time in the countryside, Geo-Caching, to try and save their relationship. Myrna is lost on the moors and COURAGE finds himself being questioned by the local police, who seem very suspicious. He tries to explain what happened.

COURAGE

I should be out there with those search teams, not sitting here having an idle chit-chat with you. How are you going to know where to look? I'm the only person who was out there with her, the only one who has the faintest idea where she might be and you've had me in here for over two hours answering stupid questions and drinking your piss-water tea! You call yourself police? Anyone with half an eye could tell how much I love Myrna, you can ask anyone in the village too, her parents, the woman in the local pub – ask anyone! I love her with all my heart...and she's out there in that... That fucked-up place on her own... (COURAGE *starts to break*.) I can't believe this... It was meant to be a time for reconciliation... This break away from London was I mean... She told me she wanted us to make a go of it, spend some time alone with no distractions so we could patch things up, you know? Are either of you married? You must have had some bad times right, some times when you doubted the relationship? Well that's the space that we were in... Well, she was anyway. I didn't have the slightest doubt in my mind that I loved her. I felt that way since the moment I first laid eyes on her, has that ever happened to you? Saw her and thought she was the one. Then... Then this other person came in the frame and it threw me for a moment, I'll admit that it threw me... But that feeling in my heart never died. I was just waiting. Waiting to see if it could be rekindled in her heart. And it's strange, because even though she kept telling me it was, I only had to look into her eyes and I could see... There was no fire burning there any more. (*Laughs bitterly.*) Not even any smoke, know what I'm saying? We were out on the moor, lost doing this fucking GPS thing, supposedly trying to save our relationship and in the middle of all that...this third party calls... Or texts, whatever... But she makes contact. And that's when I had to let go, do you understand? 'Cause I asked her, you know, I said, 'What d'you want to do?' and she just looks at me and said, 'I don't know,' but when I looked into her eyes I saw that she did. And I still loved her, my fires were still burning, yet she couldn't even face me let alone speak. So I left her. I left her out there on the moor by herself and there's nothing I can do about that now. If I had the choice of taking back one thing I've done in my life, just one wrong move I'd made, that would be the one. But I can't. She's gone and there's absolutely nothing I can do about it...

PART THREE: THIRTIES

From

LIFE AFTER LIFE
by Paul Jepson and Tony Parker

Life After Life *was first performed at the National Theatre Loft in London in May 2002.*

This play is a dramatic piece of reportage, which draws on interviews with murderers attempting to rebuild their lives. ALAN is currently doing a life sentence for murdering a policeman. Here, he explains to the interviewer exactly what happened. The interview takes place in the prison store room.

ALAN

I'd broken into a jeweller's shop in a shopping arcade in one of those new towns about midnight. Got in round the back and thought I was clever that I hadn't set the alarm off. Didn't know it was one of that new type though did I? Don't make a sound, work by infra-red and show up on the monitor in the security office. They press a button and a police patrol car's there in two minutes flat, you've not had any warning yourself at all. The first I heard's just a slight noise at the back, the same way I'd come in. I thought, 'There's something here I don't like, I'm off out of this.' Step outside into the alley, and there's this young copper standing there with his torch. 'All right you,' he says, 'let's be having you, you're nicked.' I gave him a shove to get past him, then I started to leg it away as fast as I could. Apparently he radioed a short message for assistance and then set off after me. I ran out on to a path, it was dark but there was moonlight: I could see it was by a stream and there was a wood over the other side. I'd no idea how deep it was but I jumped in and the water only came to just somewhere about here over my ankles. He jumped in after me: right determined he was. When I got the other side I turned round, and we both stood there facing each other. I remember it very clearly: weird it was. The moonlight, this fair-haired lad quite a bit smaller than me, both of us standing there panting. He'd lost his helmet in the chase. I could feel there were stones under my feet and I bent down and picked one up. He wasn't scared; like I said, very determined, he just came on. I hit him on the head with the stone, and he went down on his face in the water.

I didn't stop to see how badly he was hurt, I was up the bank and away as hard as I could. Shit-scared.

From

GLADIATOR GAMES
by Tanika Gupta

Gladiator Games *was first performed at the Crucible Studio in October 2005 and transferred to the Theatre Royal Stratford East in November 2005.*

On the night of his release from Feltham Young Offenders Institution, Zahid Mubarek, a young British Asian, was murdered by his racist cellmate. Zahid had been sentenced to 90 days imprisonment for the theft of six pounds' worth of razor blades and interfering with a car but his killer had a prison career spanning nine years and a history of racist violence. *Gladiator Games* traces the Mubarek family's pursuit of the truth. IMTIAZ AMIN is Zahid's uncle and only ten years older than him. The following monologue was reproduced from an original interview with IMTIAZ. He speaks directly to the audience.

IMTIAZ

Apparently from the court (*Hesitates.*) … Tanzeel told me
that when he was there – it was quite poignant looking back
on it now – in hindsight because it was like when the Judge
said 'take him down' or whatever, Zahid just turned round
to his grandad and Tanzeel and said in Punjabi, *'Me jara ow'*,
it was his way of saying, 'I'm going again'. He said just the
expression on his face was, was, you know, er, it was like…
they was never going to see him again. You know…er…

Long pause

At the time, my nephew and my dad thought it was pretty
much the way they deal with things here. And especially
dad, he believes in the system. My father's point of view was
look – he's going to the Young Offenders Institute – it's not
a full-blown prison. They've got to have things in place to
rehabilitate er… (*He laughs sadly.*) have things in place to sort
them out so that they can lead a more productive life. Had
we known this much (*Measures a speck with his fingers.*) of
what Feltham was about, really, you know, it would have been
different. It would have been different. I was in Holloway
Prison a couple of weeks ago, a visit for the prison law course
I'm doing and I met a prison officer there. He said to me, 'You
look remarkably familiar', and so I told him my name. He
put his arm around me and said: 'Look, I'm really, really sorry
about what happened. I was working at Feltham at the time
and I knew Zahid. He was a smashing lad.' This was just a
couple of months ago – it really hit me.

He was very much loved – despite his problems. He was very
much loved.

From

2 GRAVES
by Paul Sellar

2 Graves *was first presented at The Pleasance Theatre,
Edinburgh in August 2006 and transferred to the Arts Theatre,
London in November 2006.*

JACK is a hardened criminal who is seeking revenge for his
father's death. His story is told to the audience in the form
of a contemporary verse monologue. JACK's father, Bobby
Topps, was close to winning the 1978 Professional Darts
Championship but was forced to throw the match by gangsters
who threatened to kill JACK. Bobby (supposedly) killed himself
when he failed to win a second contest and found himself in
debt to the gangsters. JACK is drawn into London's underworld,
ostensibly to pay off his father's debts, but also to avenge him.

He ends up in prison for a murder he didn't commit.

JACK

Ever wondered why so many villains on the street talk out the corner of their mouths?

Habit from prison where you're not allowed to talk
So you learn to talk without getting caught

'Don't turn round.'

Blimey.

It's Alf. Alfie Bates.
One of my old man's mates

'You're Bobby's boy ain't you?'
It's him all right.
'Don't say nothing son. Say nothing to no one.
Nothing at all.'
'But this time next week a few of us are going over the wall.'

Well blow me –

I was made up – fuck parole
I'm getting out on my own terms
I sat around with my feet up
I walked with a roll

I'm not saying I was sure I'd make it
I wasn't. Couldn't be. 'Course not. No.
But I was just happy to be trying
Just glad to be having a go

Next few days we put it all together
Each of us have our part to play

Mine was to cause a scene

Then a van'll come in and take me off to Broadmoor. Only I won't end up in Broadmoor. 'Cos Range Rover number one will come out the bushes and smash the fucking prison van into a ditch at 40 miles an hour. Range Rover number two takes me home.

I'll keep a low profile for a while
Change of name
See my Mum straight and then who knows?
There's options…
Maybe a pub or a bar in Spain
That's the plan…
And we can do this
And we know we can

12:45 – Lunch
And I move to the front of the queue

2645. Line! Back of! Now!
Eh?
You heard. Back. Now.
'You bastard screw.'
'What did you say?'
'Nothing'
'Did you call me a bastard?'

So now I'm in control

I walk slowly to the back of the queue
Like I'm supposed to do
It's all part of my role

I don't say anything

I just smash my fucking tray across the silly bastard's face
Again and again and again

From nowhere it kicks off

Other cons are in on it and they turn over a table

Chair lock a door

We get up on our feet. Chanting and stamping

'Go! Go! Go! Go! Go! Go! Go! Go!'

From

TALKIN' LOUD
by Trevor Williams

Talkin' Loud *was first performed at the Latchmere Theatre,*
London (now Theatre 503) in February 2004.

Talkin' Loud explores the choices available for young black men
in our inner cities. Joshua and CARL are brothers and live on
a London estate. Joshua is studying and exploring his musical
talent – the world seems as though it's at his feet. However,
the stress of being attacked at gunpoint changes everything for
him. Joshua's older brother CARL is in deeper trouble. He used
to be a celebrity boxer but has fallen into a life of crime. Here,
he describes to Andrea, Joshua's tutor, how the fighting started
and how he feels about it all now. Later, we learn that he has
just killed a man in self-defence.

CARL

The man that prowls the estate like he owns it. Him and his
dog, keeping us in check. The man we all wanna take out. I
do, me little Carl. One day when he's got no dog wid him, one
of my spars decides to say something. Next thing I'm on the
floor. My spars run off and left me and I'm there on the floor
not knowing what's happened. And down there I swear I hear
something. Like nothing I've ever heard, like all the thoughts
in my head got words for them all at once. It's drilling through
my skull louder and louder like…God's thunder or…then
I'm on him thumping him, lick after lick. He can't touch me
now cos all I'm hearing is…laughter from thunder. I beat him,
beat him bad but the words all gone now, just calm and sweet.
Next day I'm somebody, the yout' that's mashed down big
man. He can't look at me again and everyone else is looking
at me different. That's the start. Soon I'm going out looking
for it, now I've got something, something that says who I am.
And I'm feeding up, getting fat on it, not listening to no one.
Mum don't know what to do wid me, school can't control
me, I don't know what to do wid me but the same time I'm
enjoying it, all eyes on me. The army, that's where I learn to
fight proper, discipline and street boy. I fight for them, in the
games, turn professional, make a bit of money. I get my fingers
in a few pies I wouldn't know how to bake myself. I'm up
there, visible, where I wanted to be. Then people start looking
at yuh a different again now, specially yuh friends. They know
yuh, remember from when yuh were all together but it's
different now. Yuh've got things, been places. It don't matter,
this is the one place that feels like home. Yuh can, they can't.

So a lot want to pull yuh down, smiling at yuh but the same time wanting to get yuh, scratch whatever it is yuh got that makes yuh so special. And…it's all just noise, in yuh head outside yuh head. How do yuh make it go away so it don't keep coming back at yuh louder?

LOVE AND MONEY
by Dennis Kelly

This play was first performed at The Studio, Royal Exchange Theatre, Manchester, in October 2006.

Set in contemporary London, *Love and Money* explores how money (or the lack of money) has an impact on love and relationships. DAVID is conducting a romance by email, with Sandrine, a French colleague whom he met at a company conference. DAVID's wife committed suicide and Sandrine has asked him to tell her about it. However, he has a shocking admission to make.

DAVID

January twenty-third.

Okay.

I came home and she was lying on the bad and she'd taken –

Pause.

I'd been test driving this Audi. It was silver. It had ABS breaking, climate control, satellite navigation and roll bar as standard. It had these little push out trays for your drinks and things. It was a lovely car. I loved it. It really held the road

Beat.

well, and the thing was the bloke who's doing the test drive, you could just tell he was thinking 'you fucking waste of my time.' But the thing was I could afford it, but

Beat.

It felt so good that car. It felt like I'd earned that car, after the things I'd been through, the things I'd

done

it felt like that car was my right.

But we had debts. Big debts. My wife had debts.

You see, he could see that I couldn't afford the car. Do you understand? It was visible on me. He could see it on me.

Pause.

So when I came home and saw her lying there I thought

I'll be able to afford the car now.

   Beat.

You don't have to email me back.

From

THE CASTLE
by Howard Barker

The Castle *was first performed by the Royal Shakespeare Company in 1985 at the Barbican Pit in London.*

STUCLEY is a knight who has returned home after fighting in the Crusades for seven years only to find that his community has created a new society, where women are treated as equals and the church has been abolished. Krak, an engineer and prisoner brought back from the Crusades, suggests building a massive castle to reinstate the men's authority. In this speech STUCLEY explains to his wife how the thought of her kept him going throughout the war and tries (unsuccessfully) to draw her back to him.

STUCLEY

I found the church bunged up with cow and bird dung, the place we married in, really, what –

Pause.

So I prayed in the nettles.

Pause.

Very devout picture of young English warrior returning to his domain etcetera get your needle out and make a tapestry why don't you? Or don't you do that any more?

Pause.

Christ knows what goes on here, you must explain to me over the hot milk at bedtime, everything changes and dreams are bollocks but you can't help dreaming, even knowing a dream is –

Pause.

It is quite amusing coming back to this I was saying to the Arab every hundred yards I have this little paradise and he went mmm and mmm he knew the sardonic bastard, they are not romantic like us are they, Muslims, and they're right! Please put this on because I –

Pause.

This wedding thing, you were sixteen years my senior and a widow and I trembled, didn't I, and you said, do not feel you must do anything, but may I kiss you I have always loved your mouth WHY WON'T YOU PUT IT ON.

Pause.

So there we were thinking – it is not a desert, actually, it is full of fields and orchards the Holy Land – and some said tell my old lady I was killed and married Arab women or Jewesses, some of them. Fewer were killed than you might think, much fewer, after all we left with fifty and it was tempting, obviously, but I thought she – wrongly it appears – she –

Pause.

Have children in two continents, most of them. Not me, though. Not in one, alas.

Pause.

I thought the time had come to – it was meant to be two years, not seven, but you know – or perhaps you don't – how wars go – coming back was worse than anything – what we did in Hungary I would not horrify you with – they got more barmy by the hour. Not me, though. I thought she'll take my bleeding feet in her warm place, she'll lay me down in clean sheets and work warm oils into my skin and food, we'll spend whole days at – but everything is contrary, must be, mustn't it, I who jumped in every pond of murder kept this one thing pure in my head, pictured you half-naked on an English night, your skin which was translucent from one angle and deep-furrowed from another, your odour even which I caught once in the middle of a scrap, do you believe that, even smells are stored, I'm sorry I chucked your loom out of the window, amazing strength comes out of temper.

From

TOAST
by Richard Bean

Toast *was first performed at the Royal Court Theatre Upstairs, London, in February 1999.*

Set in 1975, *Toast* tells the story of one night in a Yorkshire bread plant, where seven men come together to bake enough bread to feed the population of Hull. LANCE is in his mid-thirties and, supposedly, a mature student of social and economic history. The plant is one man short so he has been brought in, temporarily, to fill the gap. Here he is speaking to Walter, known as 'Nellie', who at fifty-nine has been worn down by a lifetime of making dough. Is LANCE speaking the truth or is he just a man with mental problems from the local institution, lost in a world of his own making?

LANCE

Would it be possible to touch you for a cigarette?

I normally eschew the weed, on health grounds naturally, but in situations like this the pressure of social conformity is greater than my will to live.

I'm using 'will to live' there as a figure of speech naturally – having raged unsuccessfully against the dying of the light several years ago.

I'm not a student Walter. I'm not at school. I'm here to see you. I can't tell you Walter, being dead has made a significant difference to my life. I have no concerns about my health, and I groom less. (*Beat.*) It is very opportune for me – being 'on a smoke' whilst you are taking your half hour. Alone in the canteen. It is quite perfect. One might even say designed. I feared that I would have to corner you in the lavatory or steal thirty seconds in the mixing room, just to be with you.

    Pause.

Are you prepared Walter?

How can one prepare? Death is the only real adventure. Planning, preparation, making ready – all tosh! A willing acquiescence with fate is all that one can reasonably contribute. (*Beat.*) I have told them but they take very little notice of me. I said take him, snatch him away, suddenly. Why go to the expense of sending a messenger? Do you realise, Walter, to send me here has required eight signatures on two separate requisitions. One for the exceptional expenditure incurred, and one for a four-day visa.

It is true that I am chosen for this role because I am, so I understand, perceived to be mildly eccentric, but that is functional. The living dismiss me as a madman, leaving only my clients to take me seriously. And you, Walter, are a client.

I'm a messenger. Your time is up, Walter. They've made a decision at last. An all-night meeting. A compromise solution was suggested which, though not ideal, did not damage the long-term objectives of either party. There's a place for you now. Provision has been made. Your er…loyalty to this company, and all-round contribution to society, albeit in the narrow area of bread mass production, served you well. The committee actually calculated how many loaves you've mixed in the forty-five years you've worked here. Two hundred and twenty million. That's an awful lot of toast Walter!

They're very pleased with you. All that bread! Ha! It's a mountain Walter! The decision, in the end, was unanimous – a very rare thing. The committee are already discussing the merits of another case. Walter, trust me, it's not as terrible as it sounds. I know where you're going. It's not perfect, but it could be worse. Let's just say, there are more ovens here – comprenez?

You are going to die Walter. Tonight. It'll be quick, and thankfully, there'll be hardly any mess.

From

ROOM TO LET
by Paul Tucker

Room to Let *was first performed at the Chelsea Centre
Theatre, London, in May 1999.*

ROGER is a 33 year old electrician from Swansea in South Wales.
Since his mother died he has been scouring the country for
trace of his father who walked out on them when ROGER was
nine years old. Finally, he finds him and wants him to pay for
the pain he caused. Eddie is living with his long term partner,
Janet, and ROGER rents a room from them and bides his time.
When Janet is out at work the horror begins. ROGER ties Eddie
up and lets him know exactly what it was like growing up
without a father.

ROGER

You'll never be able to make up for what you've done. At
school, the kids called me a bastard, I used to dread it,
walking through those big black metal gates in the morning
where they would be waiting for me, the sky would be yellow
and grey and you wunt believe how low I was for a nine-year-
old. They would tear my hood off my coat or hit me with
their belts when the teacher wasn't there, or they'd gob in my
face or make me lie in dogshit, if they didn't call me a bastard,
they called me flea bag or lurgy or leper. Mum couldn't afford
new clothes, so I never told her about the rips in my trousers
or in my coat, I would sit in my bedroom and sew them up
myself. Everyday, I thought you might come back, I would
imagine you walk up that garden path and you'd look up and
see me at the bedroom window and as you'd come through
that front door, things would be normal again. The sun would
come back, Christmas would be a time to look forward to and
I would never have to hear mam crying downstairs all the time
and listening to that fucking song every five minutes. But you
never came did you? You never walked up that path did you?
You just walked right out of our lives, gone, as if you never
existed, as if we didn't either. I wanted to find you, I wanted
to see what you had to say, it was heart-breaking to watch her
die, it killed me Eddie, it really fucking killed me. And where
were you? You weren't by her bedside, you weren't holding
her hand, you weren't telling her everything's gonna be okay
and God'll look after her. But the more hurt I felt then, the
more I would make you pay, and now I don't have to cry
anymore. Because it's your turn now, Eddie, it's your turn to
do the crying.

From

A NEW YORK THREESOME: MY BROTHER'S CONVERSION

by Lesley Ross

My Brother's Conversion *was originally commissioned by the Royal Welsh College of Music and Drama and first performed at the Bute Theatre, Cardiff, in July 2002.*

This is the first monologue in a trilogy called *A New York Threesome* that focuses on three very different people and the impact they have on each other's lives: SAM, his wife Bronwen and his gay brother Davey. *My Brother's Conversion* is SAM's story. In it he explains the difficult relationship he has with his brother although it was through him that he met his American wife. Bronwen was Davey's room mate in New York (where Davey was trying to establish himself as an actor but ended up in a drag act) and when SAM came to stay, he immediately fell in love with her. They married and settled in England, where SAM was a doctor. However, there was a terrible car accident and SAM has been left in a vegetable like state. Davey moved in to help, which means performing the most intimate tasks for SAM. SAM wishes he could tell him how much he truly loves him. In this part of the monologue the audience learns for the first time about the accident and its consequences. The entire monologue is spoken directly to the audience.

SAM

I was exhausted. I had been on nights, and had hardly been able to keep my eyes open during the meal, only perking up for the show, and now in my melancholic state, my eyes were once more falling heavy.

'All right, love, you drive.'

By the time we were on the M25 I had a headache; I'm going to have to sit down and relive this aren't I? I can't even remember what happened. I can't even relive it properly because I was half asleep, my mind was drifting to somewhere in nod land and I just opened my eyes when I heard the noise. There it is. There it is. Can you hear that? What is that? That's the sound of an alarm clock. No. That's a siren. No. It's the sound of something that's not right. It's telling me to open my eyes. And so I do, but we're not going straight any more. This is not the way to drive a car. And then there is a noise and a spinning and my head feels like there's a hook tearing through it and then we stop!

   Pause.

And I can see nothing, for what seems like a small lifetime, but then my brain sends an electrical message to some nerve ending in my head. Open your eyes.

Open your eyes. And eventually the eyelids respond by opening. Her face is looking at mine. Her cheeks, naturally rouged, have blood running down them and it's coming from her head and yet she seems terrified for some reason and I don't know why. I don't know what has happened. Then her brain sends a message to her, and her lips part and I think she will tell me that she loves me.

And my brain is telling me something but I don't know what it is, and in spite of myself, my eyelids start to close. And there is nothing once more.

Does anyone know exactly what a head trauma is? Do any of you even watch *ER*?

In an MVA, or an RTA if you're English, and the head is smashed in, and bleeding, and the head trauma is being seen to in the ER, we just see the faces of the nurses and the doctors, trying to save a life. We see the grief-stricken spouse struggling with all these feelings of guilt and blame while coping with their own, less severe injuries. Yet we still don't really know what's going on in the brain of the patient.

It's an amazing thing the brain, we have so little knowledge of what it can do, and yet what little knowledge we have is stored within it. So when we call someone a vegetable, we really don't know at what level he or she is functioning. Perhaps when they are in that state, when they seem like an abstract painting of themselves, perhaps they are utilising more of that brain than we ever imagined possible, that in that dream world, that other existence they have returned to, they are really superheroes, or god-like beings, or simply a younger version of themselves, stood on a stage, performing for their own abstract painting of an audience.

And so Davey is moving in, to help with the vegetable. Me.

From

A NEW YORK THREESOME: MADAM BUTTERFLY'S CHILD

by Lesley Ross

Madam Butterfly's Child *was first performed at the Hong Kong Fringe Club in January 2000.*

This is the second monologue in a trilogy called *A New York Threesome* that focuses on three very different people and the impact they have on each other's lives: Sam, his wife Bronwen and his gay brother DAVID. *Madam Butterfly's Child* is DAVID's story. In it he explains all about his experience as Second Japanese Villager From The Left in a production of *Madam Butterfly* at the Royal Albert Hall and how it leads him to the possibility of a new career as a theatrical child chaperone. DAVID is excited by the prospect as he hasn't made much of a success of his life. Unfortunately we (the audience) already know that this too is doomed to failure. In *My Brother's Conversion*, the first monologue in the series, DAVID's brother, Sam, refused to write him a reference for the job. The entire monologue is spoken directly to the audience.

SECOND JAPANESE VILLAGER FROM THE LEFT (DAVID)

Anyway, as you can see, I am a performer in this production of *Madam Butterfly*. I'd like to say that I'm an important role, but I'm actually Second Japanese Villager From The Left. Which means that I don't sing, I don't speak, but I am paid a respectable amount of money to fish and to whisper quietly in a cod Japanese accent. Today is the open dress rehearsal, so not only are you four thousand people, but you are actually friends, family and corporate sponsors, so could you all just go the extra mile and imagine that you got in for free. Thanks. Now, I am aided and abetted in my most exemplary version of being an opera extra by my fisherwoman mother, who is played by a half-Chinese lady called Lila. She is however Japanese Villager via Knightsbridge and our Japanese Villager ad lib conversation consists of –

'There's not many fish today, Mother.'

'No, but there's quite a lot of people in tonight, aren't there darling?', while I'm trying very hard to live through the emotions of a turn-of-the-century Japanese man.

'Today is Butterfly's wedding, mother. We must pray to the ancestors.'

'Mmm. Mmm. You know, I don't think I've seen this many people since I danced Giselle. Did you know I danced Giselle?'

I could see our turn-of-the-century conversations were going to be difficult. Talking to Lila in the real world was hard enough. She had this awful habit of not finishing sentences, and then just staring off into space.

'Yes, you see when I was working with Angela Rippon, she said that I needn't have bothered with the...'

One of life's true eccentrics. Although also an extra herself, she claimed to have at one time been a great opera singer. I have never made such a claim. I can only claim to have been a failure in most everything I put my hand to. You see to supplement my meagre income as an actor, I had tried everything. I tried being a waiter. Failed. Tried being a disc jockey. Failed. And this very afternoon, prior to my gig at the Albert Hall, I had failed at becoming a sperm donor. No, seriously. You lot are very good at multiplying yourselves. But my sperm. No. You see, I, like two percent of the male population in Britain, suffer from Azoospermia. Zero sperm count. David's sperm: nil points. And nil points was pretty much how I was feeling coming into the Albert Hall.

The lights fade in the audience. Madam Butterfly, *Puccini's opera, begins.*

Music. There's the music. Oh, I love this bit. That moment in the theatre when the lights go down, the audience is seized with anticipation, and something wondrous is about to begin. And we're in the Royal Albert Hall. Think of the people who have performed here. The Royal Ballet. The London Philharmonic. Even Bananarama. And now me.

And here we are, me and my fisherwoman mother, watching Pinkerton, the American sailor preparing to take a Japanese wife. I turn to Lila to try one final attempt at living in the past.

'Look, mother, look at big eyes. So funny, mother, so funny.'

'It's not funny that my second husband divorced me. It's not funny that someone tried to blow up the underground yesterday. Is it? Is it!'

'Ah yes, Butterfly's wedding. Ancestors. Ah-sa-sa-sa-sa-sa.'

I decide it's better to just steer clear of any conversation with my remarkably Western-sounding mother and concentrate on my fishing.

From

HARVEST
by Richard Bean

The first performance was at The Royal Court's Jerwood Theatre, London in September 2005.

In 1875, Lord Primrose Agar, wagered 82 acres of his land that his dog would outlive one of his tenant farmers, 94 year old Orlando Harrison. Thirteen years later the dog died and Orlando became a landowner. *Harvest* is the story of the Harrison family's continual struggle to keep hold of the land. The play starts in 1914 after Orlando's death and his two sons, William and ALBERT, argue over who should go to war and who should stay at home to look after the farm. The next scene takes place in 1934 and we learn that William lost both his legs in the war and ALBERT is married to Maudie, who was once his brother's sweetheart. ALBERT and Maudie are unable to have children and, the question of who will tend to the farm (and land) after they've gone, haunts ALBERT. It almost drives him to stealing a baby from the hospital where his niece, Laura, was born. He tells his brother the story.

ALBERT

I dint go straight to the farm sale. I went up to the hospital.

Aye, I climbed ovver the 'ospital fence, went through the gardens. I knew where to go cos that's where Katie had her little Laura. There was a side door open and I went in and it's just after dinner time and I teks me hat off, and smiles at the mothers like I'm a dad, and I just have to gerrout cos I can feel me face just burning up, and I'm in a corridor and there's a side room and I can see there's a bain in theere and the mother's asleep. Little lass, couldn't be more than sixteen, bonny but summat common about her. Mebbe she wan't wed and that's why she were in that room, I dunno. I have a look see if the bain is a boy. He is. I pick him up and he dunt cry or owt. I walk out.

ALBERT stands and pours himself a whisky, then sits.

Never been one for this stuff. It's alright. I picked the bain out the cot…and headed straight out across the gardens with 'im. I gorr half way across and there's this nurse, a sister I think, bit aulder, sitting on a bench and she stands and ses, 'Hello.' Just like that. 'Hello.' And I ses, 'How do?' – and she ses, 'D'yer want me to tek that bain off yer hands?' and I ses, 'Aye,' and I gives her the little bugger and she looks at me and it was like them auld eyes of hers is looking deep down into my soul, and me face is burning up again, and I climb the fence and I run to the hoss and I'm away.

ALBERT drinks.

I can see why some folk can get accustomed to this stuff.

He tops up his drink, and drinks again.

He was a fine, dark looking boy, despite his mother. I think he woulda ended up being a good, big lad. Aye, well. I don't think she was a country lass though. She'd be Beverley or Hull mebbe.

Fastest way of losing this land is having no-one to work it.

From

THE EDITING PROCESS
by Meredith Oakes

The Editing Process *was first performed at the Royal Court Theatre, London, in October 1994.*

'Footnotes in History' is an obscure academic journal that has been swallowed up by a large publishing company. Not only has its offices been relocated to Acton but some of the staff face redundancy and a desperate battle for survival ensues. LIONEL is 39 years of age and wields a great deal of power as the general manager of the parent publishing company, boasting 'I've terminated three publications this afternoon'. He has just propositioned Ted, the ambitious assistant editor of 'Footnotes in History' but speaks this monologue directly to the audience.

LIONEL

My life is losing all credibility. I'm tired. I hate being tired.
I'm doing this to prove I'm not tired, which I am. As for
my work. The owner is a man who has fads. This publishing
company's a fad, he made his money in sunbeds but now he's
more interested in the leisure market. Last year his fad was
management training and he sent me off for a week's survival
in Scotland. Twenty-four middle management hay fever
sufferers abseiling down a Scottish cliff. Holding a rope in one
hand, clutching an inhaler in the other one. Gasping like fish.
The course was run on military lines. Never apologise, never
explain. The commanding officer would pose with his foot on
a rock and quote Kipling. In shorts. Imitating battle conditions
as closely as possible. Men prepared to risk their lives are
first in line for promotion. Our activities were exhausting and
pointless, no-one was told what anyone was doing and there
were no decent shops for miles. I definitely found it relevant
to my work. It's a shame about my survival team of six. The
course was devised to make us form an effective unit based on
trust and we did, but I'm the only survivor now, I've sacked
the rest.

From

TRAGEDY: a tragedy
by Will Eno

A reading of TRAGEDY: a tragedy *was first held at the Royal National Theatre Studio in June 2000 and first performed at The Gate Theatre, London, in April 2001.*

TRAGEDY: a tragedy is a tongue-in-cheek exploration of the media's coverage of tragic events. JOHN IN THE FIELD represents the dashing, perfectly groomed reporter on the scene of a tragedy, covering events for the television audience at home. In the play, night-time has fallen. Will the sun ever rise again? JOHN IN THE FIELD reports to Frank in the Studio and speaks to the camera.

JOHN IN THE FIELD

It's the worst world in the world here tonight, Frank. People are all over, everywhere. Or, they were. Some, hopelessly involved with the grief here at the scene. Still others, passersby to the suffering, slowly passing by, looking, feeling, hoping and believing that they might learn something from these dark times, that they might find some clue about living, hidden in the dusk of the faces of those who have seen so much so fast, and such sadness.

Something is out there, or in here, and this is what we are watching. Or being watched by. One man came by a moment ago, and then, I felt, could not go on. We did all we could to keep him and his hope up until, after a time, his sister arrived, who had seen him wandering on her television, in the background behind me, in her living room at home. When she came and saw him here, she said, "There you are." He smiled. So that was one touching moment in an evening which has been largely bereft of the nice touches normally associated with the soft nights of this season.

Another thing I should say is, just, what an incredible job the animals have been doing out here tonight. You can perhaps see in my background the dogs going back and forth. They have been barking at the dark and generally doing those things they can usually be counted on to do, and these include: licking hands, yawning, circling before lying down, and making their tags and collars jingle. This, of course, all, as the hours grow more and more late out here, and we, it seems, learn less and less. That's what we know so far. Frank?

PART FOUR: FORTIES PLUS

From

HE LEFT QUIETLY
by Yael Farber and Duma Kumalo

He Left Quietly *was written and created by Yael Farber in
collaboration with Duma Kumalo and was first premiered
in Berlin and afterwards at the National Arts Festival in
Grahamstown, South Africa, in 2002. It is published alongside
of* A Woman in Waiting *and* Amajuba: Like Doves We Rise *in*
Theatre as Witness (*three testimonial plays from South Africa
which were created with and based on the lives of the casts
performing them*).

He Left Quietly explores the story of DUMA KUMALO who was
sentenced to death for his alleged participation in the murder
of a town councillor in Sharpeville, South Africa during the
Apartheid regime. Three years later, DUMA and his co-accused
(who became known as the 'Sharpeville Six') were given a stay
of execution fifteen hours before they were due to be hanged
because of pressure from the international community. DUMA
spent a further four years in prison and was released in 1991.
Despite his efforts, including a hunger strike and the desperate
act of destroying a court room with an axe, the case was never
re-opened and his name was never cleared. He died in 2006 at
the age of 49.

This speech occurs at the beginning of the play. He walks
slowly towards a chair, lights a cigarette and sits. He looks at
the audience and holds a silence with them. At the peak of the
tension created by the silence, he exhales a cloud of smoke,
nods and quietly begins.

DUMA

When does the soul leave the body?... At which precise
moment?

Does it leave with our last breath?... Or the final beat of our
heart?

Is it possible that I stayed here amongst you – the living – long
after my soul quietly left my body behind?

In my life I have died many times. But here I am again and
again – alive.

I am Duma Joshua Kumalo. Prisoner Number V 34 – 58.

In 1984 I was condemned to death for a crime I did not
commit.

I spent three years on Death Row, and a further four years
of a Life Sentence. I have been measured for the length of
my coffin; the size of the rope for my neck; I took my last
sacrament; I said – to my broken father – a final goodbye.
(*Smiling gently.*) And with each of these moments, my soul
left my body behind. The dead leave the living with a burden.
When going to their deaths – they would shout to us: Those
who survive – tell the world!

Pause as he looks at the audience.

I speak for them.

They live in me.

Perhaps it is they who are talking when I open my mouth.

I cannot undo the past.

I cannot change what happened to me.

And so I live with what I have seen – on borrowed time.

In a chanting style, reciting his traditional praise names.

Duma hamba uyoDuma ezizweni – uNoDumo uhleli kaMenzi.
[Go Duma and be famous worldwide...]

Life is mystery.
The road turns in ways we could never imagine. I took the
wrong road one morning... And never came back the same
man.
Who would I have been if I had not taken that road?
Impossible to say...
Because from inside Death Row – you find your own voice
before you die. You see your own truth.
You finally understand the meaning of your own name.
Duma Joshua Kumalo.
V 34-58.

From

13 OBJECTS
(The Investor's Chronicle)
by Howard Barker

---

13 Objects, *directed by Howard Barker, opened at the Birmingham Rep in October 2003.*

A collection of thirteen short self-contained plays explore how people make emotional (and sometimes disturbing) investments in inanimate objects. In *The Investor's Chronicle* we find a rich man who is threatening to burn a Holbein painting that he's just bought at auction.

MAN

I'm burning it

Pause.

I think
I try to be honest
I think
Even as I bid for it
As I lifted my fingers off my knee
(I love those auctioneers they see the slightest movement it
might have been a nod but I just lift my fingers off my knee)
I knew it would be burned by me
Yes
The blood rushed to my face
My heart beat quicker and this wasn't nerves this wasn't
the anxiety of bidding in a public place the thrill of the
accumulating figures
(This went in tens of thousands incidentally)
It was my terrible desire rising
It was my animal leaning on its chain

Pause.

They were all
Oh it was pitiful
All after it the thin curators the dribbling collectors even
yes an actor in dark glasses I don't know his name a million
women wet themselves for him an American I don't know his
name he sat stone still he was acting probably he never stops I
left him far behind I left him at a million and a half he got up
silently and silently he left he had no curiosity he had to make

a film a million and a half so much for his love of art I smiled
I particularly resent the proximity of actors actors belong in
restaurants I permitted myself one thin smile

> *Pause.*

Holbein

> *Pause.*

Holbein

> *Pause.*

1553

> *Pause.*

And it isn't as if I don't know art
Oh
The
Contrary

> *Pause. He takes out a hip flask, unscrews the top and
> sprinkles whisky over the painting.*

Holbein is my favourite
Twenty years I waited for him
AND THE PUBLICITY
I won't quote
BILLIONAIRE RECLUSE
That's me
PAYS FOUR-POINT-FIVE MILLION FOR
Oh these figures get me down what do they know about art
it's arithmetic to them the more noughts on the end the more
appreciative they are
CONNOISSEURS MY

> *He takes out a cigarette lighter.*

ANUS

Pause. He ignites a flame.

Holbein

Pause.

1553 they say I've got my doubts he was in Ghent in 1553 and yet the subject is an Englishwoman of course he could have travelled or so might she but 1554 is more accurate in my opinion but let the experts always let the experts let them let them I say

He is about to put the flame to the picture but stops.

And the frame's nice
The frame is pear inlaid with ivory
Which won't burn obviously
The ivory
Only the pear
The ivory

Pause.

I'll kick that into the flower bed

Pause, then he lets the flame snuff out.

I hate them all
I hate
I hate them all

Pause.

Not Holbein
Oh no
Not him
THOUGH HIM I MIGHT HAVE IF WE'D MET
I don't rule it out

A snob he was no doubt

He might have peered at me down his long nose he might

have revealed under those heavy eyelids a contempt for me

Pause.

I hate them all but

Pause.

And I try to be honest

I do try

Pause.

That is not the reason I am burning it

I'M NOT A SCHOOLBOY

WHAT DO YOU TAKE ME FOR SOME SNOTTY

VANDAL SPRAYING HIS NAME ACROSS A BROTHEL

WALL

I AM A BILLIONAIRE

Pause.

It said so in the papers

Pause.

I am burning

Not

A

Painting

No

Oh

No

I am burning all the human filth who make this painting no

longer a painting at all

From

WHAT THE NIGHT IS FOR
by Michael Weller

What the Night is For *was first produced by Act Productions,
Sonia Friedman Productions and LHP at the Comedy Theatre,
London, in November 2002.*

Ten years after the end of their affair in New York, ADAM and
Lindy meet in a bland Midwestern hotel room for dinner. Both
are in their mid to late forties and married with children but
their passion for each other hasn't died. The night reveals their
hopes, dreams and regrets. In this speech, ADAM explains that
he would like their feelings for each other to evolve into a long
term secret affair.

ADAM

We vowed we'd always have each other while the rest of our life went on. It was a marriage, Lindy. A secret marriage.

I've thought a lot about that idea over the years. More and more in fact. What a good thing it might have been –

My partner's dad comes to town on business three times a year and once up in Riverdale way off the beaten path, inspecting a job site, I saw him go into a restaurant with his arm around this plump smiley white haired lady with pink cheeks, you know, wire rim glasses, one of those jolly-sexy older liberal lady types. Herman turned and saw me. He's married, you see. I know his wife. She's great. They're a total family-family. My partner still thinks growing up with them ruined his chances for marriage because he'll never be as happy with someone as his folks are with each other, and it's true, they're happy. But there's his old dad – oh, right; six months later he treated our office to dinner, he's in town *with his wife* this time, and when I go in the men's room he's right behind me, boom, to the next stall. 'The woman you saw me with, we've been lovers for thirty-seven years. No one knows, not even my kid, you got that?' and he walks out. I found him back at the table with his arm around his wife…he loves her, too. Herman is an ordinary guy. Husband, provider – solid citizen. It's *not* a fairy tale.

I want you back.

From

SCENES FROM THE BACK OF BEYOND
by Meredith Oakes

*This play was first performed at the Royal Court Jerwood
Theatre Upstairs, London, in November 2006.*

BILL lives in a new Sydney suburb at the end of the 1950s.
He is in his forties with a wife and fifteen year old daughter.
Despite some reservations about his life he believes the world
is improving and that the only thing the human race needs to
do is learn. In this speech he tries to explain to his daughter,
Jasmine.

BILL

When I was a kid about his age, our friends had this holiday shack

It was set back from the beach behind the dunes, and the grass around the shack was adorned in all directions with cow dung

I remember standing in the doorway thinking, this is a bit unsavoury

When suddenly the father of the family picks up a cow-pat and buzzes it at the mother and she catches it and buzzes it back at him

And the next thing that happens, the father, the mother and me and kids all together are running around chucking cow-pats at each other

Having the time of our lives

The weather was so dry down there, they'd dried out like meringues

They were the best thing to throw I ever threw

And it struck me with the force of a vision. These people knew something my family and I didn't know

How to live

I've been hoping ever since it's something you can learn

And pass on, so the microcosm feeds into the macrocosm and the macrocosm feeds back into the

Do you see what I mean?

It's finding how to make things, I don't know

It's finding things are really OK

From

A HOLE IN THE FENCE
by David Foley

A Hole in the Fence *was first performed at the White Bear Theatre, London, in a production by Box of Tricks Theatre Company, in association with Joabri Productions Ltd and the White Bear Theatre Club in June 2007.*

The play is set on a US naval base in Newport, Rhode Island in 1919. MR VOLE is in his forties and a Chief Machinist's Mate. He has been entrusted by the Navy to clean up 'homosexual practices' within the ranks because of his previous experience dealing with vice in the Connecticut State Police. He recruits three young sailors to infiltrate the 'scene'. In this monologue, he briefs the sailors to work undercover, have sex with any homosexual sailors they meet and provide him with a written report on what has occurred. The sailors are standing in formation with their backs to the audience as MR VOLE addresses them.

MR VOLE

You all know why you're here. Each man among you has been recommended as a sailor of upstanding character, moral correctness, and devotion to the service of the Navy.

Pause. He takes a solemn breath.

Gentlemen, we stand upon a sink of vice such as would make a Roman emperor blush. Do you know what vice is, gentlemen? It's a disease. Allow it a purchase and it will spread, infecting the healthy and debilitating the body of the state itself. Every mother sends her boy to the Navy hoping we'll send her back a man, a man trained in the highest ideals of the republic. Well, every mother's son here is in danger: in danger of infection from this gross, disfiguring disease. The solemn duty we take upon ourselves today, the solemn oath we make to that faraway mother pining for her boy, is to strain every sinew in our bodies, expend every ounce of our courage, to root out this pernicious plague.

Your duty, to put it plainly, is to obtain information about and evidence against the cocksuckers and rectum receivers who are plying their infamous trade in the very bowels of the United States Navy. To do this you must enter the dens of vice itself. You must pretend to be one of them, make free with them, be jolly and good-natured, make assignations, and allow yourselves to be taken into their confidence.

Every morning before ten hundred hours, you will submit a report typed in quadruplicate. Reports should be detailed and frank and should include the names and ranks of each suspect as well as where they live and where they are stationed.

Is there anyone now who wishes to be dismissed from these duties?

No one moves.

Brave men! I leave you with these three words: Infiltrate. Penetrate. Report.

Dismissed.

He salutes.

From

NIGHTS AT THE CIRCUS

by Tom Morris and Emma Rice
(adapted from the novel by Angela
Carter)

This adaptation was first performed in January 2006 at
the Lyric Hammersmith in London, produced by the Lyric
Hammersmith and the Bristol Old Vic in association with
Kneehigh Theatre.

The nineteenth century is drawing to a close and Fevvers, a
girl with wings from the East End of London, joins the circus
as a trapeze artist. She is pursued by a journalist, Jack Walser,
who wants to prove she is a fraud but gradually falls in love
with her. He is given a job at the circus as the 'jam face' or new
clown. BUFFO is the chief clown but has a vicious streak: he
regularly beats his mistress, Mignon. Prior to BUFFO's speech,
Jack is attacked by one of the circus' tigers whilst trying to save
Mignon. BUFFO is cradling JACK whilst he speaks.

BUFFO

Let me tell you a story.

I was in Copenhagen when I had the news of the death of
my adored mother, by telegram, the very morning on which
I buried my dearly beloved wife who had passed away whilst
bringing stillborn into the world the only son that ever sprang
from my loins.

All my loved ones…dead.

But that afternoon at matinee time at the Tivoli, I dragged
myself into the ring and tumbled and fell – how they roared
with delight.

And then – in a moment – I looked up at all the grinning faces
and I froze…like a baby gasping for air. And they laughed.

'I can't go on!' I screamed at them. 'My heart is broken!' And
they still laughed. And I drank in their laughter.

After the show, I scrubbed off my clown's face and staggered
to a bar in the thickest part of the town. And I drank and I
drank until I didn't know who I was.

I wanted to drink in the entire world and piss it out against a
wall.

And a barmaid turned to me and said, 'It can't be that bad.'
'Oh but it is,' I said. Then she gave me some advice. 'Take
yourself along to the Tivoli this evening. Have a look at Buffo
the Clown. He'll put a smile on your face,' she said. 'He'll put
a smile on your face.'

Scrape off these faces and what do you find?

Despair. Failure. And Pain.

The crowds laugh at our failure. They love our humiliation. The greater the humiliation, the greater the clown.

That is why we are top of the bill, my friends. That is how we keep the circus alive. They love our pain. And our pain redeems them.

So you see a clown is like Jesus looking forward with bright eyes to his martyrdom.

But as they sit there in heaven, do they laugh when he falls? Would we laugh if we got there too?

From

LIFE AFTER SCANDAL
by Robin Soans

Life After Scandal *was first performed at Hampstead Theatre, London in September 2007.*

Classified as 'verbatim theatre', *Life After Scandal* is a series of intertwined interviews with people who have been involved in public scandals, including Jonathan Aiken, Edwina Currie, Craig Murray, Neil and Christine Hamilton, and, Charles and Diana Ingram. The play explores how people survive public humiliation and investigates a whole industry built on shame. MENAJI is part of the paparazzi but is able to see how ludicrous his job actually is.

MENAJI

Here we are…it's the beast…it's a Canon…it's a tool of the trade…it's a bit of a beast. I'm a paparazzo, but I'm not telling you my name. My camera does eight and a half frames a second, it's all digital…forget film, film's great, but too much aggravation… (*To BARMAN.*) …I'll have a beer…

Anything as long as it's not crap… (*To us.*) …it's a 2.8 70-mil to 200-mil zoom with auto-focus…now that means you only want the one lens…that's vital, you don't want to be fucking about changing lenses in the middle of the action. You don't carry a camera bag cos then everyone knows you've got a camera…you have a bag that looks like any sort of bag…you don't have any bits with you; you won't be far from your car…you can have all your shit in the car.

For your more powerful shots, you need a tripod, but usually in that kind of situation you're in a bush, or up a tree, on the beach, or behind a wall looking onto the beach.

So this is a zoom lens, good for a low light, and you can put a doubler on this if you want to get in close. You spend a lot of time outside someone's house, we call it the location, and you have to be there early before they leave.

There's always paparazzi cruising in their cars, following someone as they go about. Look, look at this…I was at an actress's house, outside her house, couple of hours ago…on a scout…followed her home on the off-chance…you never know who's gonna turn up…photographed this girl who turned up…don't know who she is…could be anybody…she didn't know I was photographing her…out the window of my car...scratching her thigh look...running her hand through her hair...look at this one...checking her mobile phone. Following is always better. I went through twelve red traffic lights in a fortnight following Kate Moss...there may be other paparazzi following her...you don't want them getting 'the shot'. What you want is an exclusive. If someone's snorting cocaine or picking their nose, I'll leave that alone, but a lot of photographers are looking for that...crack-sweaty-arse-pants-zoom in on armpits, all sorts of crap. You only ambush someone if it's going to be difficult following them, or there's a back entrance out of a building and you can't cover it.

The ambush is when you jump out in front of them and blitz them. The cry is 'Go, go, go', and we all jump out.

You won't be quoting this under my name will you? They fucking do whatever they want to do whenever they want to do it. They buy the photographs off me, and then they just make up the headlines and the captions underneath...the story underneath is nonsense.

From

TALKING TO TERRORISTS
by Robin Soans

Talking to Terrorists *was commissioned by the Royal Court Theatre and Out of Joint Theatre Company. It was first performed at the Theatre Royal, Bury St Edmunds in April 2005.*

Talking to Terrorists portrays ordinary (real) people who have been involved in extraordinary events, including terrorists, hostages, survivors, politicians, journalists and psychologists. The writer, director and actors interviewed people from around the world who had been involved in or affected by terrorism. Although it isn't stated in the play, THE ENVOY is Terry Waite who, as the Archbishop of Canterbury's Assistant, travelled to Lebanon in the 1980s to try to secure the release of four hostages and was captured by terrorists himself. He is speaking to an unseen interviewer.

THE ENVOY

I got up at something like four in the morning…'cause it was very heavy snow. I got up before the family woke and I thought, 'Well, I'll be back in seven or eight days,' and I never said goodbye to them. Only just got to Heathrow 'cause the snow was so heavy…got the plane into the Lebanon, and that was it. That was it for five years.

I took bodyguards from the airport into town and a short-wave radio so that I could pick up signals from Terry Anderson's flat, where I was staying. That evening the phone rang. 'We're the people you want to see, come and meet us,' and they named a place. Well you can't just go out and meet…it's dangerous out there. I said, 'First of all…'…yes, crikey, I'd forgotten this…this is stranger than fiction…I said, 'Before we go any further, will you give me the nickname of a girlfriend of a friend of Terry Anderson's.' I knew full well that to get that obscure bit of information they would have to be in contact with Terry Anderson or at least with one of his guards. After two hours they phoned back. 'The name's Christo.' That was the right name, and the next night I agreed to go and see them.

I went to a doctor's waiting room. He said, 'You've asked to see the hostages; we're going to let you see them 'cause they're sick and very depressed.'

I said, 'Look, if I come with you, you'll keep me.'

He said, 'We will not keep you.' He gave me his hand on this. He stretched out his hand.

I said I needed twenty-four hours to think about it. He agreed.

Really the decision had to be mine. If the hostages really were, you know, sick…how sick? What if I didn't go and one of them died?

I went back the next night. As soon as I walked in, the telephone rang. The doctor said, 'I'm sorry, there's an emergency at the hospital.' In fact he left at that moment.

I thought, 'Well, if I've come this far, I might as well go through with it, you know.'

A few minutes later my contact stepped into the room. I was given a quick body-search, we went down in the lift, got into a car, changed cars, then I was blindfolded, and we went into a safe-house. Over the next three days we moved from house to house, they said to shake off a tail; and finally, on the fourth day, I was put into a van, blindfolded, and driven across town. We came to what I believed was an underground garage. In the floor was a trapdoor. He said, 'Jump down.' The door closed behind me, and, when I took off my blindfold, I was in a tiled cell. I was no longer a negotiator…I was a hostage.

From

THE ERROR OF THEIR WAYS
by Torben Betts

The Error of their Ways was first performed in August 2007 at the HERE Arts Center, New York.

A popular politician is brutally assassinated and his beautiful but icy widow, Elizabeth, takes his place as leader. However, she feels an overwhelming desire for her husband's assassin, which threatens her future success. REVEREND DRINKWATER is a priest who drinks in order to dull the pain of his life. He desires Elizabeth and, although he would be willing to give up his vocation for her, knows in his heart that she would reject him. This speech takes place in a church and DRINKWATER is alone and drunk.

REVEREND DRINKWATER

Intoxication, I…revel in you. I plunge into your tranquilising depths and here I float as you cradle my aching soul in your most generous embrace. Oh, inebriate, oh drunkard, oh sot… (*Laughs.*) Sot. Yes, I a sot, a besotted sot, a toad, a toper, a relentless quaffer of froth, and each mouthful moves me further from you, Lord. Each swill of poison shunts me further from the truth. Each spasm of pleasure is a slap to your cheeks: your face ever severe, your look ever stern, ever condemnatory. Oh why the hell did you bring her here? Is this woman, this Satan in black stockings, this she-demon in an evening gown, this witch in widow's weeds, is she how you try my strength? You mean me to fall at the first hurdle, Lord? Oh and fall I would so happily do. Fall into her body and sink my sleek and desperate tongue deep between her legs I… I shall banish the thought and think only upon Jesus. But this, mark you, this would not be weakness. No, it would be courage, Lord. The opening of a gateway into uncharted lands. But no, I shall and I will think only upon Jesus. The Christ…the Jesus…our nailed-up Messiah. The loving protector, the innocent lamb. But you see, the other ones I can disregard. Happily. Without a twinge of it, without so much as a trembling. Others do nothing for me. Those well-dressed ladies who queue up after a sermon and ask the predictable questions: the nature of divinity, the trials upon the cross, the reasons for all this suffering, this human suffering upon an industrial scale, Lord! (*A pause.*) Forgive me. But you have seen them, yes? These simpering schoolgirls and bored-to-death housewives, these flower arrangers, these group-joiners, these committee-attenders, they bombard me, Lord. They bombard me and yes I could pluck any one of them at any time, one sideways glance and they would be peeling off stockings and taking off pearls and kicking off thigh-boots and hitching up skirts, and I could bend their unloved and unlovable bodies over this altar and I could pound like a pig and I could thrash and I could grunt, and oh how I would grunt, Lord. I have decades of grunting saved up, my sweet Lord, decades of it, bestial noises that would fill the empty chasm of this church, this hangar, this soundless vault, it would split the tiles from the roof and make the steeple shudder, Lord. Yes, our sweating bellies would slap like wet clay and our hungry dry lips they would slather like hounds, chewing and snapping in our frenzy, our mad, mad frenzy to lose our poor desiccated selves in another's stinking liquids. Oh yes, Lord. You know I could. Make those young wifies moan. But no…these are not for me. No, I want the rage and the desolation behind that woman's eyes. And how much longer can I hold out? But…she would never acknowledge me, no.

From

JAMAICA INN

by Daphne du Maurier in a new
adaptation by Lisa Evans

Jamaica Inn *was commissioned by Salisbury Playhouse and*
first performed there in April 2004.

Based on the classic novel by Daphne du Maurier, which is set
in nineteenth century Cornwall, *Jamaica Inn* tells the story of
Mary Yellan who goes to live with fretful Aunt Patience and
her oppressive husband, JOSS MERLYN, at Jamaica Inn on bleak
Bodmin Moor. Mary's mother has just died so she has nowhere
else to turn. She soon discovers mysterious things happening
under the cover of darkness but it isn't until her uncle drinks
a little too much one night that she discovers the awful truth.
JOSS is a 'wrecker' who lures ships aground on the Cornish
coast, murders the people on board and steals their cargo.

JOSS

It's a hard game Mary but they can't catch me. I'm too cunning. There's over a hundred of us now, working inland to the border from the coast. Here, come close, down here by my side, where I can talk to you. We ought to be partners you and I. I'm fond of you. You've got sense. Should have made you a boy. I shouldn't drink. I see things that never scare me when I'm sober. Damn it, Mary, I've killed men with my own hands and slept in my bed like a child.

But when I'm drunk I see their white-green faces staring at me, with their eyes eaten by fish, and some of them are torn, with the flesh hanging on their bones in ribbons. There was a woman once, Mary, she was clinging to a raft and she had a child in her arms. Her hair streaming down her back. The ship was loose in on the rocks you see, and the sea was as flat as your hand. They were all coming in alive, the whole bunch of them. She cried out to me to help her, and I smashed her face in with a stone. She fell back, her hands beating the raft. She let go of the child and I hit her again. I watched them drown in four feet of water. We were scared then. For the first time we hadn't reckoned on the tide. In half an hour they'd be walking dry shod on the sand. We had to pelt at them all with stones, Mary, break their arms and legs. And they drowned there in front of us because they couldn't stand.

Did you ever hear of wreckers before?

The clock strikes the half hour.

The sound of it rings in my head sometimes, like the tolling of a bell buoy in a bay. Travelling down the air on the westerly wind. Backwards and forwards the clapper goes against the bell as though it tolled for dead men. It rubs on your nerves and you want to scream. When you work the coast you have to pull out to them in a boat and muffle them. Wrap the tongue in flannel. There's silence then. Maybe it's a misty night, with patches of white fog on the water, and outside the bay there'll be a ship casting for scent like a hound. She listens for the buoy, and no sound comes to her. And she comes in then, driving through the fog. She comes straight into us who are waiting for her Mary, and we see her shudder suddenly and strike and then the surf has her. Have you ever seen flies caught in a jar of treacle? I've seen men like that. Stuck in the rigging like a swarm of flies. They cling there for safety, shouting in terror at the sight of the surf.

Just like the flies they are, spread out on the yards, little black dots of men. I've seen the ship break up beneath them, and the masts and yards snap like thread, and there they'll be flung into the sea to swim for their lives. But when they reach the shore they're dead men Mary. And they say nothing.

From

ROUSSEAU'S TALE
by David Pownall

This play was first performed at The Cockpit, Marylebone, London in October 1990 as part of the Not The RSC Festival.

Rousseau's Tale is a monologue spoken by the eighteenth century French revolutionary philosopher, JEAN-JACQUES ROUSSEAU. It is an imaginary exploration of a supposed lecture given by ROUSSEAU to the Royal Society in London on the subject of his sexual feelings.

ROUSSEAU

There was a time when I was about nine when I was boarded out to be fostered by a pastor, Monsieur Lambercier, to study Latin and all the rubbish that masquerades as education. I was a lively boy but I do not believe that there has ever been a child with less vanity. I worked hard at my lessons but fell short of expectations and the pastor's sister resorted to physical chastisement. When I was thrashed I discovered that the experience of being beaten by a mature woman was not entirely unpleasurable and it came to pass that I would contrive mischief in order to be assailed by Mademoiselle Lambercier, with whom I fell in love.

The confusion that exists here between the law and sex is clear. The lack of care that the pastor took in determining the rightness of my punishment created a conundrum in my childish mind.

I have argued to myself on my long, lonely journeys into exile, that I have spent my life seeking the opprobrium of those set in authority because it gives me pleasure, not because I disapprove of their methods of government. However, it was a boy of nine who responded in that way. I was unafraid, excited, willing to be aroused by pain. If there is a lesson in later life it is surely that: to make use of pain and never waste suffering.

I should add that when the pastor himself beat me there was no pleasure in it at all. As Mademoiselle Lambercier became exhausted, or aware of my delight, she passed the responsibility for my chastisement increasingly to him.

My response was to become better behaved so corporal punishment won the day, but it was a hollow victory. If the persecutions that I endure ever reach their ultimate stage and my life is forfeit I imagine that I will go to the gallows as a groom to the bridal bed.

Death to the lover of political pain is, in the words of Shakespeare, a consummation devoutly to be wished.

From

THE LAST DAYS OF MADALYN MURRAY O'HAIR, IN EXILE
by David Foley

This play was first presented by the Lark Theatre Company as part of their BareBones season in New York in December 1998. The first full production was at the Ohio Theatre, New York in February 2003.

The Last Days of Madalyn Murray O'Hair, in Exile imagines an alternative conclusion to the real-life disappearance of the notorious American atheist, Madalyn Murray O'Hair. In this version of events, Madalyn has fled the U.S., with her granddaughter and one of her sons, to an island in the South Pacific. OMOLU is in his late fifties and is one of the natives of the island. He is described as 'clear-eyed and serene, with a courtly manner and a slightly British clip to his speech', probably from his time at university in England. In this speech, OMOLU explains Madalyn's death to his own son, Hank, Madalyn's granddaughter, Rita, and Madalyn's other son, Jim, who recently arrived on the island.

OMOLU

There comes a time when one must decide between telling the truth, however unpalatable, or piling prevarication upon prevarication until you yourself can no longer see where you first strayed from the path of complete veracity. I believe this is one of those moments when nothing will serve but the bald truth. Mrs. Jones is dead because we killed her.

She suffered very little pain. Last night – under the influence of a very strong potion the making of which has fortunately not passed from our diminishing store of folkloric knowledge – surrounded by worshiping and dancing men and women – garlanded in flowers and brightly painted – Mrs. Jones' throat was slit over a ceremonial basin whose original devising is now shrouded in the mists of ancient history.

Yes, it's all very complicated. We live, I need hardly tell you, in difficult times. What does this island seem like to you? A resort? A getaway? A tropical paradise? I see it otherwise. I look around me, and I see among my people all the ills of the modern age. Alcoholism, violence, immorality, alienation, crime, and most of all that terrible, dislocating despair – that hopelessness – that is the besetting evil of our times.

It was not always so on this island. Before we were introduced to the advantages of Western culture and the profits of Western tourism, we had our own way of life and our own beliefs. Perhaps they would strike you as primitive, backward, but they kept us united, ordered, and as happy as anyone can expect to be in this vale of tears to which each of us is consigned for the brief span of a human life.

We worshipped at that time a goddess. Such things, as you know, vary from culture to culture, and ours was the volcano goddess. Perhaps because our ancestors, in their simplicity, saw in the volcano a powerful instrument of life and death. And as in most primitive societies, our goddess lived among us. She rose among us, as one of us. A woman of powerful personality, possessed of a kind of demonic fire – she would become the goddess. And she was worshipped and glorified. And when the time came for her to die – for all gods must die – she was killed, with tears and jubilation, so that she could live again – in another woman. The goddess is dead, long live the goddess.

Needless to say, it is a long time since the goddess has lived among us. But as I considered the societal problems that I have just outlined for you, I realized that we needed her among us again. To unite us in that most precious thing – a shared belief. And so I began to look for a goddess for my people. A powerful woman. A monstrous woman. A woman of deep and unholy urges. And then, as if she'd been sent for, your mother arrived.

Ah, I have left out one small detail. In order for the goddess to remain among us, we must partake of her holiness. We must – *ingest* her.

From

BLUE EYES AND HEELS
by Toby Whithouse

This play was first performed at Soho Theatre in London in October 2005.

Blue Eyes and Heels satirises the world of commercial television. Duncan is an ambitious young producer, searching for the next 'big thing' in order to make his name. He plans to bring wrestling back to British television and draws in VICTOR, who at 55 is one of the old guard. VICTOR used to play the role of villain, wearing a mask as *The Count of Monte Cristo*, and was quite a name in his day with regular touring. He is desperate to reclaim his original glory and, in this speech, tries to explain the appeal of the sport to Duncan.

VICTOR

It's funny, going round the country, on the train, in the Allegro, it used to give me time to think. I'd read as well. I've read all sorts. Books about Churchill, mythology, computers, but mostly I'd just think. See, with the Wrestling, people are always saying, 'It's fixed!' But that's missing the point. No one watches – I don't know – 'Hamlet' and says it's fixed. It doesn't matter if we know who's going to win, it's how we *get there*. *That's* the entertainment. People want to see struggle. Even if it's not real, they want to see it because that's what their life is. Only, in life, you go through stuff, and you go through it on your own. You can't always scream, you can't always shout or use your fists. When your wife – you can't fall apart. So you'd go to the Wrestling. The Greeks understood it. That's why they'd go to their tragedies. To see something... *played out* in front of them, something what's usually private. And the Wrestling was so *simple*. These battles, everything was so basic. And I don't mean it was crude. I mean it was black and white. Good people and bad people, Blue-Eyes and Heels. There wasn't any – you knew if someone was evil coz they had bloody great mask on. (*Laughs.*) You've got me started now.

And the power we'd generate, the the the the *fury*, as we'd control the audience, manipulate them. One minute the hero's got the advantage, then all of a sudden the Heel pulls some stunt, something wicked, and *he's* got the upper hand. And the audience can't do anything! They just have to sit and watch! And they're screaming because they want the ref to stop the fight, just to *look*, but he's not paying attention! It's – I even thought of a name for it. Delicious Agony. Coz that's what it is. The villain's pulling a fast one and the audience can only sit and watch. Do you know what I mean?

From

THE POSSIBILITIES
(Only Some Can Take the Strain)
by Howard Barker

The Possibilities *was first performed in 1988 at the
Almeida Theatre in London.*

A collection of ten short plays explore some disturbing moral
dilemmas and ambiguities in different times and cultures. THE
BOOKSELLER in *Only Some Can Take the Strain* is described as
an 'ageing man' with a 'handcart laden with books.' He risks
arrest by selling controversial, possibly banned, books in a police
state. Here, we find him talking to the audience.

BOOKSELLER

Usual wind on the embankment. Usual unkind wind.

Pause.

Usual bird shit on the volumes. Usual unkind birds.

Pause. He wipes the books.

I railed at the birds. I railed at the wind. But I was young, then. Now I say, shit on! Blow on!

Pause.

Usual fumes from the motor cars. The ever-increasing torrent of motor cars. Our arteries are clogged with anxiety, our lungs are corroded with fumes. WHAT A CONSPIRACY AND NOBODY KNOWS EXCEPT ME. We are out of control, oh, so out of control.

He shuffles the books.

Yesterday I sold a book. To be precise, I took money and surrendered a book. This was certainly what is commonly known as a sale. Unfortunately, or fortunately, since not every setback appears so on reflection, hardly had the customer left the stall when for some obscure reason I shall never understand, he turned on his heel and replacing the book, asked for his money back. I said, you do this to torture me! But thinking this over during the night, I have concluded that this peculiar action was, in the most general sense, beneficial, since I have the book still in my stock and consequently the knowledge it contains remains in safe hands. I regard it as a bookseller's mission to be cautious regarding who might get his hands on stock.

Pause. He fusses.

Of course this cannot last. This will not be allowed to last. THEY WILL ACT. Both I and the books will be ELIMINATED. I have lived with this for years. I knew, as if by intuition, that time was short. I knew we would be burned. The books burned, and the booksellers also. You think the stake was something of the Middle Ages? No, they shall be my pyre, and I, their pyre. OH, SOMEHTING HAS SHIT ON THE BOOKS!

He pulls out a dirty cloth, rubs a volume.

Oh, we are out of control, so out of control…!

A figure has appeared who stares at the BOOKSELLER. The BOOKSELLER is aware.

Police.

He rubs on.

I act dishevelled. I act the tramp. This way I avoid the attention of both criminals and police. This way the cart appears to be a cart of junk and not, as it is, a pantechnicon of truth which might lever up the world.

From

LIES HAVE BEEN TOLD: AN EVENING WITH ROBERT MAXWELL

by Rod Beacham

Lies Have Been Told *was first produced by Philip York, who performed the play, and Rod Beacham, who directed it, in August 2003 at the Edinburgh Fringe Festival. It opened in October 2005 at the New End Theatre, London, and subsequently transferred to Trafalgar Studios in the West End in January 2006.*

The play explores the life and death of the infamous media mogul, ROBERT MAXWELL, who, at seventy years old, tells his own version of the events that led to his rise and fall in a monologue addressed to the audience. He was originally born in 1939 Czechoslovakia as Jan Ludwik Hoch and here he tells the audience about how he escaped from the Nazis as a Jewish refugee with the help of a Czech gypsy.

MAXWELL

Did you ever wonder how I got out of Czechoslovakia? When the Nazis came pouring in? How I didn't end up dead or in a concentration camp, instead of fighting side by side with the British Tommy? I'll tell you. It's a good story, you'll enjoy it.

Of course the bastards did get me. Grabbed me off the streets. Do you know I can't even remember what they arrested me for? Not that it really signifies, because the real charge was being a Jew. Only in those days it wasn't quite that simple, they still hadn't officially made it a capital offence, so they trumped up some charge or other and threw me in a cell. And kept me there for three months, waiting for my trial. Three months. And they beat me up every day. Every day for three months, they came into my cell and beat the crap out of me. Nothing too heavy, of course, they didn't want me dead, that would have spoiled the party.

And do you know what the stupid bastards did then? All right, I was only sixteen, and I was weak enough when they grabbed me, let alone by the time they'd finished with me, but I was big, for Christ's sake, I was a big bloke even then. And the silly sods sent me off to court handcuffed to a single guard. And the poor bugger only had one arm.

I don't know how he lost it, I asked him as soon as we were on the train, but he was a sulky bastard, he never did tell me.

So. There we are, him and me in a carriage to ourselves, joined at the wrist. And at the last minute, the train had actually started when the door opens and this gypsy woman throws herself into the carriage. The guard tried to order her out, but she made out she didn't understand him, and by then it was too late, we were up and running.

She was glorious that woman. A real Czech gypsy, dark and glorious. I've always thought that the world is divided into two sorts of people: those who think you're insulting a woman when you say she looks like a gypsy, and those who think you're paying her a compliment. I've always belonged firmly to the latter camp. Anyway, she sat down, and our eyes met, and something happened in that split second. Of course there was bound to be a sympathy between us, those cold juiceless bastards hated her people as much as they hated mine; life, fire, passion, they hated it wherever they found it, it scared the shit out of them. But it was more than that, it was personal, as soon as our eyes met I knew I'd found a friend.

After that it was simple, I just wrapped my free hand round the little bastard's throat, and held him there with his eyes popping, while she got the key out of his pocket and undid my handcuffs.

The Books

HELMET
by Douglas Maxwell

ISBN 978-1-84002-275-9

PRIVATE PEACEFUL
by Michael Morpurgo,
adapted by Simon
Reade

ISBN 978-1-84002-660-3

MANCUB
by Douglas Maxwell

ISBN 978-1-84002-475-3

OSAMA THE HERO
by Dennis Kelly

from *Plays One*

ISBN 978-1-84002-803-4

RISK AND VIRGINS
by John Retallack

from *A Company of
Angels*

ISBN 978-1-84002-725-9

BLUE
by Ursula Rani Sarma

ISBN 978-1-84002-269-8

CROSSFIRE
by Michel Azama,
translated by
Nigel Gearing

ISBN 978-1-84002-34-7

FAITH
by Meredith Oakes

ISBN 978-1-870259-80-4

PLAYING FIELDS
by Neela Dolezalova

ISBN 978-1-84002-349-7

**CRESSIDA AMONG THE
GREEKS**
by David Foley

from *The Murders at
Argos, Cressida Among
the Greeks*

ISBN 978-1-84002-323-7

THE DARKER FACE OF THE EARTH
by Rita Dove

ISBN 978-1-84002-129-5

THE GUARDIANS
by Peter Morris

ISBN 978-1-84002-642-9

CAR and KID
by Chris O'Connell
from *Street Trilogy*

ISBN 978-1-84002-389-3

A QUESTION OF COURAGE
by Courttia Newland
from *White Open Spaces*

ISBN 978-1-84002-686-3

KINGS OF THE ROAD
by Brian McAvera

ISBN 978-1-84002-390-9

LIFE AFTER LIFE
by Paul Jepson and
Tony Parker

ISBN 978-1-84002-301-5

KISS ME LIKE YOU MEAN IT
by Chris Chibnall

ISBN 978-1-84002-236-0

GLADIATOR GAMES
by Tanika Gupta

ISBN 978-1-84002-624-5

BEST MAN SPEECH
by Glyn Maxwell

ISBN 978-1-84002-615-3

2 GRAVES
by Paul Sellar

ISBN 978-1-84002-713-6

THE GOD BOTHERERS
by Richard Bean
from *Plays Two*

ISBN 978-1-84002-415-9

TALKIN' LOUD
by Trevor Williams

ISBN 978-1-84002-472-2

LOVE AND MONEY
by Dennis Kelly
from *Plays One*
ISBN 978-1-84002-803-4

**THE CASTLE AND
13 OBJECTS: THE
INVESTOR'S CHRONICLE**
by Howard Barker
from *Plays Two*
ISBN 978-1-84002-648-1

TOAST
by Richard Bean
ISBN 978-1-84002-104-2

ROOM TO LET
by Paul Tucker
ISBN 978-1-84002-125-7

**MY BROTHER'S
CONVERSION AND
MADAM BUTTERFLY'S
CHILD**
by Lesley Ross
from *The Jolly Folly of
Polly, the Scottish Trolley
Dolly*
ISBN 978-1-84002-541-5

HARVEST
by Richard Bean
ISBN 978-1-84002-594-1

THE EDITING PROCESS
by Meredith Oakes
ISBN 978-1-870259-46-0

TRAGEDY: A TRAGEDY
by Will Eno
ISBN 978-1-84002-234-6

HE LEFT QUIETLY
by Yael Farber and
Duma Kumalo
From *Theatre as
Witness*
ISBN 978-1-84002-820-1

WHAT THE NIGHT IS FOR
by Michael Weller
ISBN 978-1-84002-355-8

**SCENES FROM THE
BACK OF BEYOND**
by Meredith Oakes
ISBN 978-1-84002-708-2

A HOLE IN THE FENCE
by David Foley
ISBN 978-1-84002-790-7

NIGHTS AT THE CIRCUS
by Tom Morris and
Emma Rice

ISBN 978-1-84002-631-3

ROUSSEAU'S TALE
by David Pownall
from Plays One

ISBN 978-1-84002-076-2

LIFE AFTER SCANDAL
by Robin Soans

ISBN 978-1-84002-805-8

**THE LAST DAYS OF
MADALYN MURRAY
O'HAIR, IN EXILE**
by David Foley
from *Three Plays*

ISBN 978-1-84002-473-9

**TALKING TO
TERRORISTS**
by Robin Soans

ISBN 978-1-84002-562-0

BLUE EYES AND HEELS
by Toby Whithouse

ISBN 978-1-84002-638-2

**THE ERROR OF THEIR
WAYS**
by Torben Betts

ISBN 978-1-84002-801-0

**THE POSSIBILITIES:
ONLY SOME CAN TAKE
THE STRAIN**
by Howard Barker
from *Plays One*

ISBN 978-1-84002-612-2

JAMAICA INN
adapted by Lisa Evans

ISBN 978-1-84002-409-8

LIES HAVE BEEN TOLD
by Rod Beacham

ISBN 978-1-84002-658-0